Guitar Chord █ ░ k

P9-DDM-222

Wedding Songs

ISBN 978-1-4234-6635-2

HAL•LEONARD®
CORPORATION

7777 W. BLUEMOUND RD. P.O. BOX 13819 MILWAUKEE, WI 53213

Visit Hal Leonard Online at
www.halleonard.com

Guitar Chord Songbook

Contents

All I Ask of You

from THE PHANTOM OF THE OPERA

Music by Andrew Lloyd Webber
Lyrics by Charles Hart
Additional Lyrics by Richard Stilgoe

Melody:

No more talk of dark-ness, for-get these wide-eyed fears.

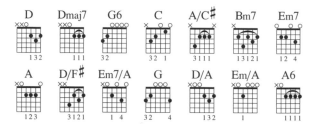

D   Dmaj7   G6   C   A/C#   Bm7   Em7

A   D/F#   Em7/A   G   D/A   Em/A   A6

Verse 1

D
Raoul: No more talk of darkness, forget these wide-eyed fears.

Dmaj7   **G6**   **C**   **A/C#**
I'm here, nothing can harm you, my words will warm and calm you.

D
Let me be your freedom, let daylight dry your tears.

Dmaj7   **G6**   **C**   **A/C#**
I'm here, with you, be - side you, to guard you and to guide you.

Chorus 1

       D   **Bm7**   **Em7**   **A**
Christine: Say you love me ev'ry waking moment,

D/F#   **Bm7**   **Em7**   **Em7/A**
Turn my head with talk of summertime.

D   **Bm7**   **Em7**   **A**
Say you need me with you now and always.

D/F#   **G**   **D/A**
Promise me that all you say is true,

Em/A   **A6**   **Em/A**   **D**
    That's all I ask of you.

Verse 2

    D
Raoul: Let me be your shelter, let me be your light.

    Dmaj7   **G6**   **C**   **A/C#**
You're safe, no one will find you, your fears are far be - hind you.

    D
Christine: All I want is freedom, a world with no more night.

    Dmaj7   **G6**   **C**   **A/C#**
And you, always be - side me, to hold me and to hide me.

Chorus 2

    D   **Bm7**   **Em7**   **A**
Raoul: Then say you'll share with me one love, one lifetime

D/F# Bm7   **Em7**   **A**
Let me lead you from your solitude.

D   **Bm7**   **Em7**   **A**
Say you need me with you, here be - side you.

D/F#   **G**   **D/A**
Anywhere you go, let me go too.

Em7/A   **A6 Em7/A D**
Christine, that's all I ask of   you.

Chorus 3

    D   **Bm7**   **Em7**   **A**
Christine: Say you'll share with me one love, one lifetime.

D/F# Bm7   **Em7**   **Em7/A**
Say the word and I will follow you.

D   **Bm7**   **Em7**   **A**
Share each day with me, each night, each morning.

D/F# **G**   **D/A**
Say you love me. *Raoul:* You know I do.

       Em7/A   **A6 Em7/A D**
Christine & Raoul: Love me, that's all I ask of   you.

Interlude

| **D** **Bm7** | **Em7** **A** | **D/F#** **Bm7** |
| **Em7 Em7/A** | **D** **Bm7** | **Em7** **A** |

Outro

         D/F#   **G**   **D/A**
Christine & Raoul: Anywhere you go, let me go too.

Em7/A   **A6 Em7/A D**
Love me, that's all I ask of   you.

Always and Forever

Words and Music by
Rod Temperton

Melody:

Al-ways and for - ev - er, ____

Dmaj7   Dm/G   A7sus4   A7   A/B   Bm7   Gmaj7   Em7   F#m7

Intro | Dmaj7 | | Dm/G | A7sus4 A7 |

Verse 1
    Dmaj7   **A/B**   **Bm7**
    Always and forever,   each moment with you

    Gmaj7   **Dmaj7**   **Em7**   **A7sus4**
    Is just like a dream to me   that somehow came true.

    Dmaj7   **A/B**   **Bm7**
    And I know tomorrow   will still be the same,

    Gmaj7   **Dmaj7** **Em7**   **A7sus4**
    'Cause we've got a life of love   that won't ever change.

Chorus 1
    A7 Dmaj7   **Em7 F#m7 Gmaj7 F#m7 Em7**
    And ev'ryday love me   your   own   special way,

              A7sus4   **Dmaj7 F#m7**
    Melt all my heart away with a smile.

    Gmaj7 F#m7 Em7 F#m7
    Take   time to tell me you really care

       Gmaj7 F#m7   **Em7**   **A7sus4 Dmaj7**
    And we'll   share to - morrow ____ to - gether.

    F#m7   **Gmaj7 F#m7 Em7**   **A7sus4 N.C.**   **Dmaj7**
    (Always forever love you.) I'll   always love you   for - ever.

              Dm/G A7sus4
    (Always forever love you.)
        For - ev - er.

Verse 2

Dmaj7   **A/B**   **Bm7**
There'll always be sunshine   when I look at you.

Gmaj7   **Dmaj7**   **Em7**   **A7sus4**
It's something I can't explain,   just the things that you do.

Dmaj7   **A/B**   **Bm7**
And if you get lonely   call me and take

Gmaj7   **Dmaj7**   **Em7**   **A7sus4**
A second to give to me   that magic you make.

Chorus 2

A7 Dmaj7   **Em7 F♯m7 Gmaj7 F♯m7 Em7**
And ev'ryday love me   your   own   special way,

                    A7sus4   **Dmaj7 F♯m7**
Melt all my heart away with a smile.

Gmaj7 F♯m7 Em7   F♯m7
Take   time to tell me you really care

      Gmaj7 F♯m7   Em7   A7sus4 Dmaj7
And we'll   share to - morrow ____ to - gether.

  F♯m7   **Gmaj7 F♯m7 Em7   A7sus4**
(Always forever love you.) I'll   always love you

N.C.   Dmaj7 Dm/G A7sus4
For - ever,   ev - er.

Outro

Dmaj7   **Dm/G A7sus4**
‖: (Always forever love you.)   :‖ *Repeat and fade*
                                                                  w/ lead vocal ad lib.

Ave Maria

By Franz Schubert

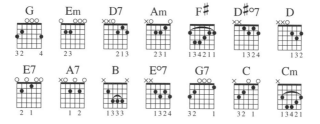

Verse 1

G Em   G D7 Em
A - ve Ma - ri - a!

Am D7 G   Em   F♯
Grati - aple - na, Maria gratia - plena,

     D♯°7   Em   D E7
Ma - ria gratiaple - na, A - ve, Ave!

      D   A7   D
Domi - nus, ___ Dominus te - cum,

       D7   G   D   Em
Bene - dicta tu in muli - erebus et benedic - tus,

    D   B   Am
Et bene - dictus, fructus ventris,

          E°7 D D7
Ventris tui, Je - sus.

G Em   G D7 G G7 C Cm G
A - ve Ma - ri - a!

Verse 2

D Em   G D7 Em
A - ve Ma - ri - a!

Am D7   G   Em   F#
Ma - ter De - i, Ora pro nobis pecca - toribus,

D#°   Em
O - ra ora pro no - bis,

D   E7   D A7   D
O - ra, o - ra, pro no - bis ____ peccatori - bus.

D7   G   D   Em
Nunc et in hora mortis, in hora mortis no - strae,

D   B   Am
In hora mortis, mortis nostrae,

E°7   D D7
In hora mortis no - strae.

G Em   G D7 G G7 C Cm G
A - ve Ma - ri - a!

Because

Words by Edward Teschemacher
Music by Guy D'Hardelot

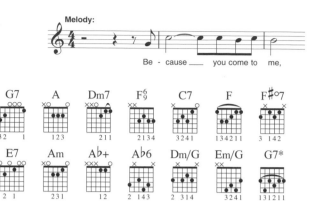

Melody:

Be - cause _____ you come to me,

Verse 1

|C| |Em| |Dm6|
Be - cause you come to me, with naught save love,

G7   A   Dm7   F⁶₉   G7
And hold my hand and lift mine eyes a - bove,

C7   F
A wider world of hope and joy I see,

F#°7 C/G G7   C Em Dm6
Be - cause you come to me.

Bridge

G7   C7   F
Be - cause you speak to me in accents sweet,

D7   Gm7
I find the roses waking 'round of my feet,

E7   Am
And I am led through tears and joy to thee,

Ab+   Dm7 G7 Dm7
Be - cause you speak to me.

Verse 2

G7   C   Em   Dm6
Be - cause God made thee mine, I'll cherish thee

G7   A   Dm7   F⁶₉   G7
Through light and darkness, through all time to be,

C7   F
And pray His love may make our love di - vine,

F#°7 C/G G7   C   Am Ab6 Dm/G Em/G G7* C
Be - cause God made thee mine.

Here and Now

Words and Music by
Terry Steele and David Elliot

Melody:

One look in your eyes,

Cadd9 D7sus4 G D/G G/B F#m7b5 B7b9

Em7 D Cmaj7 Bm7 Cm/Eb G/D D#°7

B7sus4 D/C D/F# G7sus4 Gadd2 Bbmaj7 Fmaj7

Intro

|Cadd9 D7sus4 |G D/G G G/B |Cadd9 D7sus4 |

Verse 1

G   F#m7b5 B7b9   Em7 D
One look in your eyes, and there I see

Cadd9   D7sus4   G
Just what you mean to me.

     D/G G   F#m7b5 B7b9 Cmaj7 Bm7
Here ____ in my heart   I believe

Cadd9   Cm/Eb G/D Cadd9
Your love is all _____ I ever need.

       G/B D#°7   Em7
Holding you close through the night,

     Cmaj7 D7sus4
I need you.   Yeah.

Verse 2

G   F#m7b5   B7b9   Em7   D
I look in your eyes and there I see

      Cadd9   D7sus4   G
What happiness really means.

D/G   G   F#m7b5   B7b9   Cmaj7   Bm7
 The love ____ that we share   makes life so sweet.

     Cadd9   Cm/Eb   G/D   Cadd9
To - gether we'll always ____ be.

          G/B   D#°7   Em7
This pledge of love feels   so right,

             Cmaj7
And, ooh, I need you.

Chorus 1

F#m7b5   B7sus4   Cmaj7   D/C   D/F#   G   D/F#
            Here and now, I   promise to love faithfully.

Cmaj7   F#m7b5
You're all I need.

B7sus4   Cmaj7   D/C   D/F#   G   D/F#   Cadd9
  Here and now, I vow to be one with   thee.

          D7sus4   G   D/G   G   G/B   Cadd9   D7sus4
Your love is all (I need.) ____ I need.

   G   D/G   G   G/B   Cadd9   D7sus4
Stay.

Verse 3

      G   F#m7b5   B7b9   Em7   D
When I look in your eyes   there I see

Cadd9   D7sus4   G
All that a love should real - ly be.

           F#m7b5   B7b9   Cmaj7   Bm7
And I need you more and more each day.

Em7   Cm/Eb   G/D   Cadd9
Nothing can take   your love away.

      G/B   D#°7   Em7   Cmaj7
More than I dare ____ to dream, I need you.

Chorus 2

F#m7♭5 B7sus4   Cmaj7 D/C   D/F# G D/F#
Here and now, I promise to love faithfully.

Cmaj7   F#m7♭5
You're all I need.

B7sus4   Cmaj7 D/C   D/F# G D/F# Cadd9
Here and now, I vow to be one with thee.

D7sus4
Your love is all I need.

Bridge

Cmaj7   D/C
(Starting here.) Ooh, and I'm starting now.

G   Cmaj7
I believe. ____ (Starting here.)

I'm starting right here. (Starting now.)

D7sus4
Right now because I believe ____ in your love,

G7sus4
So I'm glad to take the vow.

Chorus 3

Cmaj7   D/C   D/F# G D/F#
Here and now, oh, I promise to love faithfully.

Cmaj7   F#m7♭5
You're all I need.

B7sus4   Cmaj7 D/C   D/F# G   D/F# Cadd9
Here and now, I vow to be one with   thee.

D7sus4
Your love ____ is all I

Outro

Gadd2   Cmaj7
‖: Need. I yeah, yeah. Uh, yeah.

B♭maj7   Cmaj7 Fmaj7
Ay ah, ____ love is all   I   :‖

Gadd2   Cmaj7
Need. I yeah, yeah. Uh, yeah.

B♭maj7 Cadd9   Gadd2
Ay ah, ____   yeah.

Butterfly Kisses

Words and Music by
Bob Carlisle and Randy Thomas

Melody:

There's two things I know for sure, —

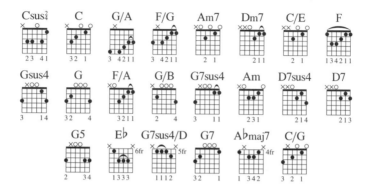

Intro

| Csus⅔ C | Csus⅔ C | Csus⅔ C | Csus⅔ C |

| Csus⅔ C | Csus⅔ C | Csus⅔ C | G/A F/G |

Verse 1

   C   Am7   C
    There's two things I know for sure,

          Am7   C
    She was sent here from heaven and she's daddy's little girl.

    Dm7   C/E   F   Gsus4 G
    As I drop to my knees ___ by her bed ___ at night,

    Dm7   C/E   F   Gsus4
    She talks to Je - sus, and I close my eyes,

    G   F/A   G/B   C   F
    And I thank God for all ___ of the joy in my ___ life.

Chorus 1

G7sus4 Csus²₄   C Csus²₄   C
Oh, but most of all for butterfly kisses ___ after bedtime prayer,

  Csus²₄   C Csus²₄ Am G
Stickin' little white flow - ers all up in her hair.

F   C/E
"Walk beside the pony, Daddy, it's my first ride.

 F   C/E
I know the cake looks funny, Daddy, but I sure tried."

  F/A   G/B
Oh, with all that I've done wrong,

      C   D7sus4
I must have done something right

D7   F   G5   Csus²₄ C
 To deserve a hug ev'ry morning and butterfly kisses at night.

| Csus²₄ C | Csus²₄ C | G/A F/G | C |

Verse 2

Am7   C
Sweet sixteen today,

  Am7   C
She's looking like her momma a little more ev'ry day.

Dm7 C/E   F Gsus4
One part wom - an, the oth - er part girl.

G Dm7   C/E F   Gsus4 G
 To perfume and make - up from ribbons and curls,

F/A   G/B   C   F
Trying her wings ___ out in a great big world.

Chorus 2
         G7sus4 Csus⁴⁄₂   C   Csus⁴⁄₂   C

G7sus4 Csus⁴ **C** **Csus⁴** **C**
But I re - member butterfly kisses ____ after bedtime prayer,

Csus⁴ **C** **Csus⁴** **Am G**
Stickin' little white flow - ers all up in her hair.

F **C/E**
"You know how much I love you, Daddy, but if you don't mind

F **C/E**
I'm only gonna to kiss you on the cheek this time."

F/A **G/B**
Oh, with all that I've done wrong

C **D7sus4**
I must have done something right.

D7 **F** **G5** **Csus⁴** **C**
To deserve her love ev'ry morning and butterfly kisses at night.

Bridge
Csus⁴ **C** **E♭**
(All the precious time.)

G7sus4/D **Csus⁴** **C** **Csus⁴**
Oh, like the wind, the years ____ go by.

C **E♭ G7sus4/D F/A** **Dm7** **G7**
(Precious butter - fly, _____ spread your wings and fly.)

Verse 3
Am7 **C**
She'll change her name today.

Am7 **C**
She'll make a promise, and I'll give her away.

Dm7 **C/E** **F** **Gsus4**
Standing in the bride ____ room just staring at her,

G Dm7 **C/E**
She asked me what I'm think - ing,

F **Gsus4**
And I said, "I'm not sure.

G **F/A** **G/B** **C F**
I just feel like I'm losing my baby girl."

Chorus 3

G7sus4   Csus2/4   C   Csus2/4   C
Then she leaned over, gave me butterfly kisses ___ with her momma there,

Csus2/4   C   Csus2/4   Am G
Stickin' little white flow - ers all up in her hair.

F   C/E
"Walk me down the aisle, Daddy, it's just about time.

F   C/E
Does my wedding gown look pretty, Daddy? Daddy, don't cry."

F/A   G/B
Oh, with all I've done wrong,

C   D7sus4
I must have done something right

D7   F   G7sus4
To deserve her love ev'ry morning and butterfly kisses.

F/A   G/B
I couldn't ask God for more. Man, this is what love is.

A♭maj7   C/G
I know I've gotta let her go, but I'll always remember

F   G7sus4   Csus2/4   C
Ev'ry hug in the morning and butterfly kisses.

| Csus2/4 C | Csus2/4 C | G/A F/G | C | ‖

Don't Know Much

Words and Music by Barry Mann,
Cynthia Weil and Tom Snow

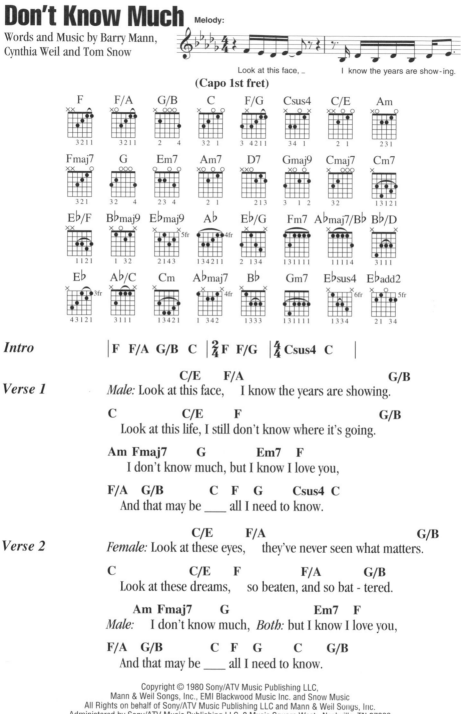

(Capo 1st fret)

Intro

| F F/A G/B C | **2/4** F F/G | **4/4** Csus4 C |

Verse 1

                            C/E   F/A   G/B
Male: Look at this face,   I know the years are showing.

  C   C/E   F   G/B
Look at this life, I still don't know where it's going.

Am Fmaj7   G   Em7 F
  I don't know much, but I know I love you,

F/A G/B   C   F   G   Csus4 C
And that may be ___ all I need to know.

Verse 2

                         C/E   F/A   G/B
Female: Look at these eyes,   they've never seen what matters.

  C   C/E   F   F/A   G/B
Look at these dreams,   so beaten, and so bat - tered.

    Am Fmaj7   G   Em7 F
Male: I don't know much, *Both:* but I know I love you,

F/A G/B   C   F   G   C   G/B
And that may be ___ all I need to know.

Bridge

        Am7   D7   Gmaj9   Cmaj7
Male: So many questions   still left unan - swered.

F   F/G   C
So much I've never broken through.

        Cm7   Eb/F   Bbmaj9   Ebmaj9
Female: But when I feel you near me   sometimes I see so clearly.

     Ab   Eb/G   Fm7
Both: The only truth   I've ever known

  Eb/G   Abmaj7/Bb Bb/D
Is me and you.

Verse 3

       Eb   Eb/G   Ab/C   Bb/D
Male: Look at this man,   so blessed with inspiration.

       Eb   Eb/G   Ab   Ab/C Bb/D
Both: Look at this soul, *Male:* still searching for salvation.

     Cm Abmaj7   Bb   Gm7 Ab
Both: I don't know much, but I know I love you,

Ab/C Bb/D   Eb Abmaj7 Bb   Eb
And that may be ___ all I   need to know.

Guitar Solo |Eb Eb/G |Ab   Bb |Eb Eb/G |Ab Ab/C Bb/D |

Outro

     Cm Abmaj7   Bb   Gm7 Ab
Both: I don't know much, but I know I love you,

Ab/C Bb/D   Eb Abmaj7 Bb   Eb Bb/D
And that may be ___ all I   need to know.

Cm Abmaj7   Bb   Gm7 Ab
  I don't know much, but I know I love you,

Ab/C Bb/D   Eb Abmaj7 Bb Ebsus4   Ebadd2
And that may be ___ all there is to know. *Male:* Whoa.

Endless Love
from ENDLESS LOVE

Words and Music by
Lionel Richie

(Capo 1st fret)

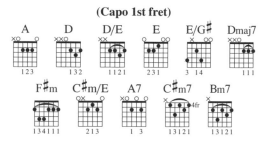

Intro |A | |

Verse 1
        A   **D**
Male: My love, there's only you in my life,

D/E   **E**   **A**
  The only thing that's right.

                       D
Female: My first love, you're ev'ry breath that I take,

D/E   **E**   **A**
  You're ev'ry step I make.

      E/G♯ Dmaj7 D/E E   **A**
Male: And I,   I want to share

       E/G♯ F♯m C♯m/E Dmaj7
Both: All my love _____ with you.

       D/E   **A**
Male: No one else ____ will do.

        A7   **Dmaj7**   **D/E**
Female: And your eyes, ____ *Male:* Your eyes, your eyes,

         E   **A**   **E/G♯ F♯m**
Both: They tell me how much you care.

C♯m/E Dmaj7   **C♯m7 Bm7**   **D/E**   **A**
Oh,   yes, you will always _____ be my endless love.

Verse 2

      A   D
Both: Two hearts, two hearts that beat as one.

D/E   E   A
   Our lives have just begun.

                             D
Female: Forever, *Both:* I'll hold you close in my arms,

D/E E   A
   I can't re - sist your charms.

       E/G♯ Dmaj7   D/E
Female: And, love, *Male:* Oh, love,

       E   A E/G♯ F♯m C♯m/E Dmaj7
Both: I'll be a fool for   you I'm   sure.

        D/E E   A   A7
Female: You know I don't mind. *Male:* Whoa, you know I don't mind.

        Dmaj7 D/E E   A   E/G♯ F♯m C♯m/E
Both: 'Cause you,   you mean the world to me. _____ Oh,

       Dmaj7   C♯m7
Female: I know *Male:* I know *Female:*   I've found *Male:* I've found

       Bm7 D/E   A   D D/E E A
Both: In you   my endless love.

Interlude

A   D
Bum, bum, bum, bum, bum, bum, bum, bum,

D/E   A
Bum, bum, bum, bum, bum.

Outro

          Dmaj7   D/E
Both: Oh, and love, *Male:* Oh, love,

       E   A E/G♯ F♯m C♯m/E Dmaj7
Both: I'll be that fool for   you I'm   sure.

        D/E E   A   A7
Female: You know I don't mind. *Male:* Whoa, you know I don't mind.

        Dmaj7 D/E E   A E/G♯ F♯m C♯m/E
Both: And, yes,   you'll be the only one

       Dmaj7   C♯m7   Dmaj7   C♯m7
'Cause no - one can deny ___ this love ___ I have in - side.

       Dmaj7   C♯m7 Bm7
And I'll give it all to you, my love. *Female:* My love, my love.

       D/E   A   D D/E E A
Both: My endless love.

From This Moment On

Words and Music by Shania Twain
and Robert John "Mutt" Lange

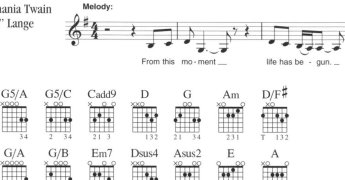

Chords: G5, G5/A, G5/C, Cadd9, D, G, Am, D/F#, C, G/A, G/B, Em7, Dsus4, Asus2, E, A, Bm, Dsus2, F#m7, Esus4, B, F#, C#m, B/D#

Intro

| G5 | G5/A | G5/C | G5 |

Verse 1

       G5   G5/A
From this moment life has begun.

           Cadd9 D
From this moment you are the one.

           Cadd9   G
Right beside ____ you is where I belong,

Am   D   G
From this moment on.

Verse 2

              G
From this moment I have been blessed.

       Cadd9 D
I live only for your happiness.

         Cadd9   G
And for your ____ love I'd give my last breath,

Am   D   Cadd9
From this moment on.

Bridge 1

      G   Cadd9
I give ___ my hand to you with all my heart.

      D/F#   C   G
I can't wait to live my life with you, I can't wait to start.

               G/A   G/B   Cadd9
You and I will nev - er be ___ a - part.

           Em7   Cadd9   G   Dsus4 D
My dreams ___ came true ___ because ___ of you.

Verse 3

           Asus2   E
From this moment, as long as I live,

      D   E
I will love you, I promise you this.

          D   A
There is noth - ing I wouldn't give,

Bm   E   Dsus2
From this moment on.

Guitar Solo | A | F#m7 | Dsus2 | E |

Bridge 2

A   D
You're the reason I believe in love,

   E   A
And you're the answer to my prayers from up above.

                    D
All we need is just the two of us.

        F#m7   Dsus2   A   Esus4 E
My dreams ___ came true ___ because ___ of you.

Verse 4

N.C.   B   F#
From this moment, as long as I live,

   E   F#
I will love you, I promise you this.

          E   B C#m   F#
There is noth - ing I wouldn't give, from this moment.

        E   B
I will love ___ you as long as I live,

C#m   F#   E B/D# F# B
From this moment on.

Grow Old with Me

Words and Music by
John Lennon

Melody:

Grow old ___ a-long with me.

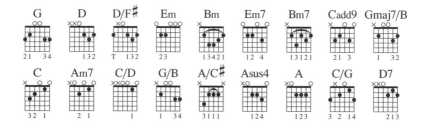

G   D   D/F♯   Em   Bm   Em7   Bm7   Cadd9   Gmaj7/B

C   Am7   C/D   G/B   A/C♯   Asus4   A   C/G   D7

Intro | G | D | | G |

Verse 1
                           G   D/F♯   G
Grow old ___ a - long with me.

                    Em   Bm
The best is yet ___ to be.

G   D/F♯   G   Em7   Bm7
    When our time has come, ___ we will be as one.

Cadd9 D   G   Cadd9 D   G
  God bless our love.   God bless our love.

Verse 2

                 G   **D/F#**   **G**
Grow old ___ a - long with me,

                   Em   **Bm**
Two branches of ___ one tree.

G   **D/F#** **G**   **Em7**   **Bm7**
  Face the setting sun when the day is done.

Cadd9 D   **G Gmaj7/B Cadd9 D**   **G**   **D/F#**
  God bless our love.   God bless our love.

Bridge

Em   **Bm**   **Em**   **Bm**
Spending our lives ___ together,   man and wife together.

C   **Am7 C/D**   **D**
World without end, world without end.

Guitar Solo

|**G**   **D/F#** |**Em** |**Am7 G/B** |**A/C#** |

|**Cadd9 D** |**Em Asus4 A** |**C**   **D** |**G** **C/G** **G** |

Verse 3

                 G   **D/F#**   **G**
Grow old ___ a - long with me.

                 Em   **Bm**
Whatever fate ___ decrees,

G   **D/F#**   **G**   **Em7**   **Bm7**
  We will see it through, ___ for our love is true.

Cadd9 D   **G** **Cadd9 D**   **Cadd9**
  God bless our love,   God bless our love.

     D   **G**   **Em7 Am7** **D**   **G**   **D D7 G**
God bless our love.   God bless our love.

Have I Told You Lately

Words and Music by
Van Morrison

Melody:

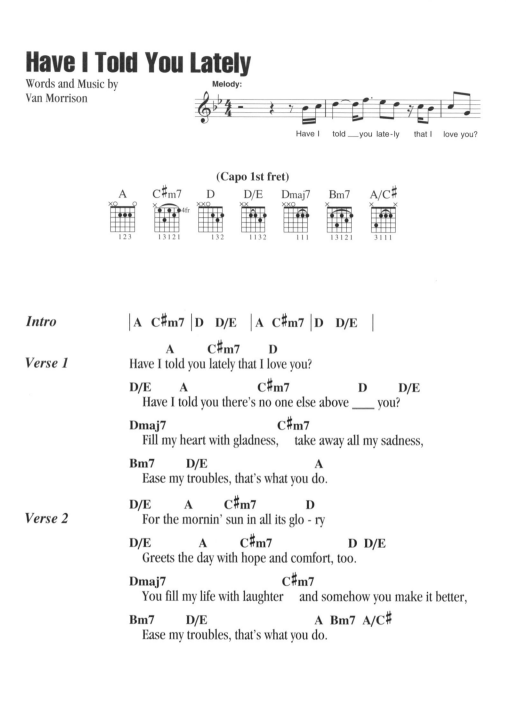

Have I told ___ you late-ly that I love you?

(Capo 1st fret)

A   C#m7   D   D/E   Dmaj7   Bm7   A/C#

Intro | A C#m7 | D D/E | A C#m7 | D D/E |

Verse 1
              A   C#m7   D
          Have I told you lately that I love you?

          D/E   A   C#m7   D   D/E
            Have I told you there's no one else above ___ you?

          Dmaj7   C#m7
            Fill my heart with gladness,   take away all my sadness,

          Bm7   D/E   A
            Ease my troubles, that's what you do.

Verse 2
          D/E   A   C#m7   D
            For the mornin' sun in all its glo - ry

          D/E   A   C#m7   D D/E
            Greets the day with hope and comfort, too.

          Dmaj7   C#m7
            You fill my life with laughter   and somehow you make it better,

          Bm7   D/E   A Bm7 A/C#
            Ease my troubles, that's what you do.

Bridge 1

Dmaj7
There's a love that's divine

                                      C♯m7   Bm7 C♯m7
And it's yours and it's mine ___ like the sun.

Dmaj7
And at the end of the day we should give thanks and pray

C♯m7   D/E
To the one, to the one.

Verse 3   *Repeat Verse 1*

Guitar Solo   *Repeat Verse 2 (Instrumental)*

Bridge 2   *Repeat Bridge 1 (Instrumental)*

Verse 4

                    A   C♯m7   D
And have I told you lately that I love you?

D/E   A   C♯m7   D   D/E
Have I told you there's no one else a - bove you?

Dmaj7   C♯m7
You fill my heart with gladness,   take away my sadness,

Bm7   D/E   A Bm7 A/C♯
Ease my troubles, that's what you do.

Dmaj7   C♯m7
Take away all my sadness,   fill my life with gladness,

Bm7   D/E   A Bm7 A/C♯
Ease my troubles that's what you do.

Dmaj7   C♯m7
Take away all my sadness,   fill my life with gladness,

Bm7   D/E   A
Ease my troubles that's what you do.

Heavenly Day

Words and Music by
Patty Griffin

(Capo 4th fret)

G   Em   C   Dsus4   Cadd9   Am   Csus2   D

Intro   ‖: G   Em |C   Dsus4 :‖

Verse 1

G   Em
Oh, heavenly day.

C Dsus4 G   Em   C Dsus4
  All the clouds blew ____ away.

G   Em C Dsus4
Got no trouble today

G   Em C Dsus4
With anyone.

G   Em
The smile on your face

C Dsus4 G   Em C Dsus4
  I live only to see.

G   Em C   Dsus4
  It's enough for me, ba - by,   it's enough for me.

               G   Cadd9   G
Oh, heavenly day, ____ heavenly day, ____ heavenly day.

Chorus 1

Em   G
Tomorrow may rain ___ with sorrow.

Am   Em
Here's a little time we can bor - row.

C   Csus2   G
For - get all our troubles in these mo - ments so few,

          Am   C
Oh, because right now the only thing that all that we real - ly have to do

D   G   Em C
Is have ourselves a ___ heavenly day.

Verse 2

D   G   Em C
Lay here and watch the trees sway.

      D   G   Em   C   D
Oh, ___ can't see no other way, ___ no way, no way.

               G   Cadd9   G
Heavenly day, ___ heavenly day, ___ heavenly day.

Chorus 2

Em   G
No one on my shoulder   bringing me fears.

Am   Em
Got no clouds up above me ___ bringing me tears.

C   Csus2   G
Got nothing to tell you, I got noth - ing much to say.

       Am
Only I'm glad to be here with you

          C   D
On this heavenly, heavenly, heavenly, heavenly,

Outro

G   Em   C   D
Heaven - ly day, ___ oh.

      G   Em C D
All the trouble gone away, ____ oh,

G   Em   C   D
For a while any - way, for a while ___ anyway.

      G   Em   G   Em
Heaven - ly day, heavenly day, heavenly day, heavenly day,

      G   C   G
Heavenly day, ___ whoa, whoa, heavenly day.

How Beautiful

Words and Music by
Twila Paris

Melody:

> How beau - ti - ful ____ the hands __

Dsus4   D   A/C#   G/B   D/F#   Em7   Asus4   A

D/A   Em7/B   F#m/C#   G   Gmaj7   Em7/D   F#m   E/G#

G/A   A/G   Gadd2   Bsus4   B/D#   Bsus4/A   B/A   G#m7

B/F#   B7sus4   B   C#m7   E   Amaj9   Esus4   B7

Intro

| Dsus4 | D | A/C# | G/B | |
| D/F# | Em7 | Asus4 | A | |

Verse 1

        D   A/C# G/B   D/A
How beautiful ____ the hands that served

      G/B   D/A   Em7/B   A/C#
The wine and the bread ____ and the sons of the earth.

        D   F#m/C# G/B   D/A
How ____ beauti - ful the   feet that walked

      G/B   D/A G/B A/C# G/B   A/C#
The long dusty roads ____ and the hill to the cross.

Chorus 1

          G   D/F# Gmaj7
How ____ beauti - ful,

A   G/B   A/C# Em7/D D
 How ____ beauti - ful,

A/C# G/B   A/C# G/B
How ____ beauti - ful

      A/C# Dsus4 D A/C# G/B
Is the body of Christ.

Verse 2

      D   A/C♯   G/B   D/A
How beautiful ____ the heart that bled,

       G   D/F♯   Asus4   A G/B A/C♯
That took all my sin and bore it in - stead.

      D   F♯m G/B   D/A
How beauti - ful the tender eyes

       G   D   G/B   A/C♯
That choose to for - give and never de - spise.

Chorus 2

        G   D/F♯ Gmaj7
How ____ beauti - ful,

   A   G/B   A/C♯ Em7/D D
  How ____ beauti - ful,

A/C♯ G/B   A/C♯ G/B
How _____ beauti - ful

     A/C♯   D
Is the body of Christ.

Bridge

D/F♯   E/G♯   G/A
And as He laid down His life,

A/G   D/F♯   Gadd2
We offer this sacrifice,

D/A   A A/G   D/F♯
That we will live just as He died,

     Gadd2   D/F♯   Gadd2
Willing to pay the price,   willing to pay ____ the price.

Verse 3

      D   A/C♯   G/B   D/A
How beautiful ____ the radiant Bride

     G/B   D/A   Em7/B   A/C♯
Who waits for her Groom with His light in her eyes.

      D   F♯m   G/B   D/A
How ____ beauti - ful when humble hearts give

      G   D   G/B   A/C♯
The fruit of pure lives so that others may live.

Chorus 3

       G   D/F# Gmaj7
How ___ beauti - ful,

A   G/B   A/C# Em7/D D
  How ___ beauti - ful,

A/C# G/B   A/C# G/B
How _____ beauti - ful,

       A/C# Bsus4 B/D# Bsus4/A
Is the body of Christ.

Verse 4

B/A G#m7 B/F# E/G# G#m7
             How beautiful

    A   E/G#   A   E/G#
The feet that bring ___ the sound of good news

     B7sus4   B
And the love of the King.

C#m7 B/D# E   G#m7 A   E/G#
        How ___ beauti - ful the hands that serve,

    A   E/G#   B7sus4   B
The wine and the bread ___ and the sons of the earth.

     A/C#   E/G# Amaj9 B
How ___ beauti - ful,

     A/C#   B/D# Esus4 E
How ___ beauti - ful,

B/D# A/C#   B/D# A/C#   B7   Esus4 E
How _____ beauti - ful _____ is the body of Christ.

Outro

|B/D# |A/C# |E/G# |
|F#m |B7sus4 B7 |E ||

I Believe in You and Me

from the Touchstone Motion Picture
THE PREACHER'S WIFE

Words and Music by
David Wolfert and Sandy Linzer

Melody:

I be-lieve in you ___ and me. ___

(Capo 2nd fret)

A   A/G   Dmaj7   F/G   G7   G   Amaj7   E/F♯   F♯m7   C♯m7

Bm7   E7sus4   Dm7   G9   D/E   Bm   Bm(maj7)   F7sus4   B♭   B♭/A♭

E♭maj7   G♭/A♭   E♭m6/G♭   B♭/E♭   Gm7   Cm7   Fsus2   A♭/B♭   B♭7   E♭/F

Intro | A | A/G | Dmaj7 | F/G G7 |

Verse 1

                A
I believe in you ___ and me.

           A/G   **Dmaj7**
I believe that   we will be in love e - ternally.

        F/G   **G**
Well, as far as I can see,

    A   **Amaj7**   **E/F♯ F♯m7   C♯m7**
You will always be the one _____ for me,

         Bm7
Oh, yes, you will.

E7sus4   **A**
   And I believe in dreams ___ again.

         A/G
I believe that   love will never end.

    Dmaj7   **Dm7**
And like the river finds the sea,

  G9   **Amaj7**   **C♯m7 F♯m7**
I ___ was lost, now I'm free

     Bm7   **D/E**   **A**
'Cause I believe in you ___ and me.

Verse 2

D/E N.C.   A
     I will never leave ___ your side.

          A/G
I will never hurt ___ your pride.

        Dmaj7
When all the chips are down, babe,

        F/G   G
Then I will always be around.

A   E/F♯ F♯m7 C♯m7
Just to be right where you are, ___   my love.

          Bm7
You know I love ___ you, boy.

D/E   A
  I will never   leave you out.

         A/G
I will always let you in, boy, mm, my baby,

  Dmaj7   F/G
To places no one's ever been.

G7   A   C♯m7
Deep inside, ___ can't you see

F♯m7 Bm7   D/E   A
  That I believe in you ___ and me.

Bridge

C♯m7   F♯m7 C♯m7   F♯m7
  Maybe I'm a fool to feel the way I do.

Bm   Bm(maj7) Bm7
I would play the fool for - ever

E7sus4   N.C.
Just to be with you forever.

Verse 3

        F7sus4 B♭   **B♭/A♭**
I believe in mir - acles, and love's ___ a miracle,

       E♭maj7   **G♭/A♭**
And, yes, baby, you're my dream come true.

  B♭/A♭ E♭m6/G♭ B♭/E♭ B♭
I, _____ I was lost,

     Dm7 Gm7
Now I'm free,   oh, baby,

     Cm7 N.C.   **Dm7 Fsus2 N.C.**   **A♭/B♭**
'Cause I   believe,   I do   believe in you and me.

   B♭7 E♭maj7   **Dm7 Gm7**
See, I was lost, now I'm free

     Cm7   **E♭/F**
'Cause I believe in you and me.

Outro | **B♭** | **B♭/A♭** | **E♭maj7 Cm7 E♭/F** | **B♭**   ‖

I Pledge My Love

Words by Dino Fekaris
Music by Dino Fekaris and Freddie Perren

Melody:

Ooh, ooh, ooh,   ooh, whee, ooh.

Gm7/C   F   Dm   Gm   C7   Am7   B♭m6

Intro

           Gm7/C
Male/Female: Ooh, ooh, ooh, ooh, whee, ooh.

Always together, together forever, always together forever.

Verse 1

      F
Male: I will love you till the day I die.

Dm
I know this now and my love won't run dry.

Gm
You came along, my life has begun.

    C7
Two hearts are now beating as though they were one.

Verse 2

      F
Female: Like the stars that make the night so bright,

Dm
You shine on me with a love that's so right.

  Gm
A love that is lasting, a love that's so pure,

C7
Each time I feel it, it makes me more sure.

Pre-Chorus 1

          Am7   **Dm**

Both: I know with all my heart we'll never part,

    Gm

For this is the day when our love comes alive,

    C7

And I mean what I say as I stand here saying:

Chorus 1

        F   **Dm**

Both: I pledge my love to you.

Gm   **C7**

  I pledge my love is true.

Am7   **Dm**

  I pledge my life to you,

  Gm   **C7**

I do, my dear, I do, my dear.

Verse 3

      F

Male: Like a river finds the deep blue sea,

Dm

Love took your hand and led you to me.

    Gm

Female: This is the "us" that I'll never forget,

    C7

Both sparkling with love, both happy we met.

Pre-Chorus 2

       Am7   **Dm**

Both: I know with all my heart we'll never part,

    Gm

For this is the day when our love comes alive,

    C7

And I mean ev'ry word and I want you to know that

Chorus 2   *Repeat Chorus 1*

Verse 4

F
Male: I'm so proud to have you by my side.

Dm
You'll be my strength and I'll be your guide.

Gm
Female: You are the one, you're a dream that is real.

C7
Heaven has sent you, it's love that I feel.

Pre-Chorus 3

Am7   Dm
Both: I know with all my heart we'll never part,

Gm
For this is the day that our love comes alive,

C7
And I mean what I say if somebody should ask me.

Chorus 3

Repeat Chorus 1

Outro

F   Dm   Gm B♭m6 F
I do,   I pledge my love to   you.

I Promise
(Wedding Song)

Words and Music by
CeCe Winans and Keith Thomas

Melody:

I could tell   by the way you __ smile, __

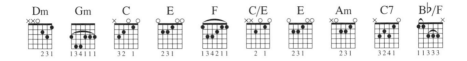

Dm	Gm	C	E	F	C/E	E	Am	C7	B♭/F
xx○		x ○○	○○○		xx○	○ ○○	x ○ ○	x○	x
2 3 1	1 3 4 1 1 1	3 2 1	2 3 1	1 3 4 2 1 1	2 1	2 3 1	2 3 1	3 2 4 1	1 1 3 3 3

Intro |Dm |Gm |C |E | |

Verse 1
             Dm   **Gm**
I could tell by the way you smile,

C   **F**
I could feel it in your ___ touch.

C/E **Dm**   **Gm**
  And I knew this heart of mine

E   **Am**   **C7**
This time would fall ___ in love. Mmm.

Verse 2
             Dm   **Gm**
All the hopes and promises given

            C   **F**
And the pain that life   can bring

C/E **Dm**   **Gm**
  Will ___ build our ___ will and commitment

       E   **Am** **C7**
To face any - thing.

Chorus 1

F   Dm   C
I will love you faithfully, for - ever uncondi - tionally,

      Gm   C
And, my love, I promise

F   Dm   C
Ev'rything I have is yours, you're ev'rything I prayed ___ and waited for.

      Gm   C   Dm Gm C F C/E
And my love I promise   you.

Verse 3

      Dm   Gm
Now we begin our life today,

      C   F
And though we've only just begun,

C/E Dm   Gm
   The quest un - til we're old and gray

    E   Am   C7
Is the vow to live ___ as one.   One, yeah.

Chorus 2

F   Dm   C
I will love you faithfully, for - ever uncondi - tionally,

    Gm   C
And, my love, I promise

F   Dm   C
Ev'rything I have is yours, you're ev'rything I prayed ___ and waited for.

    Gm   C   F   C/E
And my love I promise   you.

Bridge

Dm
Through the desert winds that blow,

Am
I'll walk you through the winters cold.

C   G
I'll be there to keep the fire   alive.

Dm
And when each passage we endure

Am
We ___ will stay strong, we can be sure

E   Am   C7 F Dm C
Our love   survives.

Chorus 3

Gm   C
And, my love, I promise

F   Dm   C
Ev'rything I have is yours, you're ev'rything I prayed ___ and waited for.

Gm   C
And, my love, I promise

F   Dm   C
That I will love you faithfully, for - ever uncondi - tionally.

Gm   C   F
And my love I promise you.

Outro

F   Bb/F F
‖: Yeah, I prom - ise you.

Bb/F   F
I'll love you for - ever and ever. :‖ *Repeat and fade*
                                      w/ vocal ad lib.

I Swear

Words and Music by
Frank Myers and Gary Baker

Melody:

I swear _ by the moon _ and the stars _

D   Bm7   A   F#m7   G/B   A/C#   G   Bm   Asus4   D/A

E/G#   Em7   G/A   Bm7/A   B7   E   C#m7   G#m7   B   Bsus4

Chorus 1

               D   Bm7   A
I swear ____ by the moon ____ and the stars in the skies.

                    D   Bm7   F#m7 A
And I swear, ____ like the shad - ow that's by your side,

Verse 1

          D   G/B   A/C#   D
   I see the ques - tions in ____ your eyes,

                    G   A   Bm
I know what's weigh - ing on ____ your mind.

                  G   Asus4
You can be sure ____ I know my part.

     A   D   G/B   A/C#   D
 'Cause I'll ____ stand beside ____ you through ____ the years,

                  G   A   Bm
You'll only cry ____ those hap - py tears.

                      D/A   E/G#   Asus4
And though I'll make ____ mistakes, I'll never break your heart.

Chorus 2
   A   D   Bm7   F#m7

And I swear ___ by the moon ___ and the stars in the skies,

       G

I'll be there.

   A   D   Bm7   F#m7

I swear, ___ like a shad - ow that's by your side,

       G

I'll be there.

  A   Em7   Asus4   A

For better or worse, till death do us part,

  Em7   Asus4   A

I'll love you with every beat ___ of my heart,

     D   Bm7 F#m7 G/A A

And I ___ swear.

Verse 2
  D   G/B   A/C#   D

I'll give you ev - 'rything ___ I can,

          G   A   Bm

I'll build your dreams ___ with these ___ two hands.

         G   Asus4

We'll hang some mem - 'ries on the walls.

  A   D   G/B   A/C#   D

And when ___ just the two ___ of us ___ are there

         G   A   Bm

You won't have to ask ___ if I ___ still care.

         D/A   E/G#   Asus4

'Cause as the time ___ turns the page, my love ___ won't age at all.

Chorus 3

A   D   Bm7   F#m7
And I swear ___ by the moon ___ and the stars in the skies,

     G
I'll be there.

A   D   Bm7   F#m7
I swear, ___ like a shad - ow that's by your side,

     G
I'll be there.

A   Em7   Asus4   A
For better or worse, till death do us part,

   Em7   Asus4   A
I'll love you with every beat ___ of my heart,

   D
I ___ swear.

Sax Solo

|Bm7   Bm7/A |F#m7 |G   A |F#m7   B7 |

Chorus 4

       E   C#m7   G#m7
I swear ___ by the moon ___ and the stars in the skies,

     A
I'll be there.

B   E   C#m7   G#m7
I swear, ___ like a shad - ow that's by your side,

     A
I'll be there.

B   F#m7   Bsus4   B
For better or worse, till death do us part,

   F#m7   Bsus4   B
I'll love you with ev'ry single beat of my heart,

    E   C#m7 A B E
I ___ swear.   Oh, I ___ swear.

The Lord's Prayer

By Albert H. Malotte

Melody:

Chord diagrams: G/B, D/A, A/G, D/F#, Em7, A, D, A/C#, F#m7*, G5, Gmaj7, Bm7, Asus4, F#m7, F#7, Bm7/A, G, C#7, D6, C#7sus4, Dmaj7, Em9, E7, D+, G6, G#m7♭5, C#7sus4/G#, Gm6, C9♭5

Intro

|G/B D/A A/G D/F# |Em7   A |

Verse

D   A/C# F#m7*   G5 Gmaj7 A
Our Father ____ which art in Heav   -   en,

Bm7   Em7 Asus4 A   D
Hallowed be _____ Thy name.

Bm7   F#m7 Bm7   F#m7
Thy kingdom come,   Thy will be done

F#7 Bm7 Bm7/A G   A/C# F#m7 D/F#   Em7 A D
In earth,   as it is _____ in heav -   en.

G/B D/A A/G D/F# Bm7 Em7 Asus4 A D
Give us   this day   our dai - ly   bread,

D/F#   Gmaj7   C#7
And for - give us our debts,

D6   C#7sus4 C#7 D6 C#7sus4 C#7
As we forgive our debt - ors.

Dmaj7   Em9 Em7
And lead us not into temp - ta - tion

E7   Asus4   A
But de - liver us from e -   vil.

D   D+   Gmaj7 G6
For Thine ____ is the King - dom,

Gmaj7   G#m7♭5 C#7sus4/G# Gm6 C9♭5 F#m7 Bm7
And the power,   and the glo - ry for - ev - er.

N.C. Em7 A G/B D/A A/G D/F# G/B D/A A/G D/F#
A   -   men.

I Will Be Here

Words and Music by
Steven Curtis Chapman

Melody:

To - mor - row morn - ing, if you ___ wake up

(Capo 1st fret)

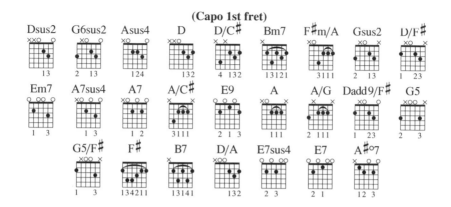

Dsus2 G6sus2 Asus4 D D/C# Bm7 F#m/A Gsus2 D/F#

Em7 A7sus4 A7 A/C# E9 A A/G Dadd9/F# G5

G5/F# F# B7 D/A E7sus4 E7 A#°7

Intro

| Dsus2 | Gsus2 | Dsus2 | Gsus2 |

Verse 1

Dsus2   Asus4 D
 Tomorrow morning, if you ___ wake up

D/C# Bm7 F#m/A Gsus2 D/F#
And the sun does not appear,

Em7 A7sus4 A7   Dsus2 G6sus2
I , _____ I will be here

Dsus2   Asus4 D
 If in the dark we lose sight___ of love,

D/C# Bm7 F#m/A Gsus2 D/F#
Hold my __ hand and have no fear

  Em7 A7sus4 A7 Dsus2 D
'Cause I, _____ I will be here.

Chorus 1

A/C♯   Bm7
I will be here

F♯m/A   E9   A
When you feel like bein' qui - et.

A/G   Dadd9/F♯   G5
When you need to speak your mind,

G5/F♯   Em7   F♯   B7
I ___ will lis - ten, and I will be here.

D/A   Esus4 E7   Asus2
When the laughter turns to cry - ing,

A/G   Dadd9/F♯   G5
Through the winning, losing and try - ing,

G5/F♯   Em7 Asus4
We'll be togeth - er,

                Dsus2 G6sus2 Dsus2 G6sus2
'Cause I will be here.

Verse 2

Dsus2   Asus4   D
Tomorrow morning, if you___ wake up

D/C♯ Bm7 F♯m/A Gsus2 D/F♯
And the future   is un - clear,

Em7 A7sus4 A7   Dsus2 G6sus2
I, _____   I will be here.

Dsus2   Asus4   D
As sure as seasons are made ___ for change,

D/C♯ Bm7   F♯m/A Gsus2 D/F♯
Our lifetimes are made for __ years,

  Em7 A7sus4 A7   Dsus2 D
So I, _____   I will be here.

Chorus 2

A/C♯   Bm7
I will be here,

F♯m/A   E9   A
And you can cry on my shoul - der.

A/G   Dadd9/F♯   G5
When the mirror tells us we're old-er,

G5/F♯ Em7
I will hold __ you.

F♯   B7 D/A
And I will be here

E7sus4   E   A A/G
To watch you grow in beau - ty

Dadd9/F♯   G5
And tell you all the things you are to me.

D/F♯   Em7
I will be here.

A7   A♯°7
Mm.

Bridge

Bm7   E7sus4 E7
I will be true

A   A/G   Dadd9/F♯
To the prom - ise I __ have made

G   D/F♯   Em7
To you and to __ the One

A7sus4 A7 Em7 A7sus4 A7
Who gave you to   me.

Outro $\mid$Dsus2 $\mid$Asus4   D   D/C$\sharp$ $\mid$Bm7   F$\sharp$m/A $\mid$Gsus2 D/F$\sharp$ $\mid$

Em7 A7sus4 A7   Dsus2
I, _____   I will be here.

G6sus2   Dsus2
  And just as sure

                 Asus4   D D/C$\sharp$
As seasons are made ___ for change,

  Bm7   F$\sharp$m/A G5   D/F$\sharp$
Our lifetimes are made ___ for ___ years.

  Em7 A7sus4
So I,

A$\sharp$°7   Bm7
  I will be   here.

D/A   Em7   Asus4 A
  We'll be together.

    Dsus2
I will be here.

$\mid$G6sus2 $\mid$Dadd9/F$\sharp$ $\mid$Em7   Asus4 $\mid$D

I've Dreamed of You

Words and Music by
Ann Hampton Callaway and Rolf Lovland

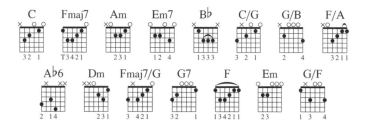

Melody:

I've dreamed of you al-ways feel-ing you

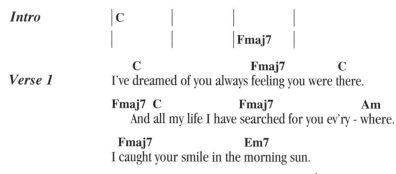

C Fmaj7 Am Em7 Bb C/G G/B F/A
Ab6 Dm Fmaj7/G G7 F Em G/F

Intro

| |C | | | | | |
| | | | |Fmaj7 | |

Verse 1

        C   Fmaj7   C
I've dreamed of you always feeling you were there.

Fmaj7 C   **Fmaj7**   **Am**
  And all my life I have searched for you ev'ry - where.

Fmaj7   **Em7**
I caught your smile in the morning sun.

Fmaj7   **Bb**
I heard your whisper on the breeze at night.

C/G   **Fmaj7**   **C**
I prayed one day that your arms would hold me tight.

Verse 2

Fmaj7 C   Fmaj7   C
And just when I thought love had passed me by, we met.

Fmaj7 C   Fmaj7   Am
That first look in your eyes, ____ I can't forget.

  Fmaj7   Em7
You melted me with your tender touch.

  Fmaj7   B♭
I felt all fear and sorrow slip away.

  C/G   Fmaj7
Now here we stand hand - in - hand

        C G/B F/A A♭6 C/G Am Dm Fmaj7/G
This blessed day.

Verse 3

  G7 C   Fmaj7   C
I ____ promise you, as I give to you my heart,

Fmaj7 C   Fmaj7   Am
That nothing, nothing in this world ____ shall keep us apart.

  Fmaj7   Em7
Come happily, ever after

  Fmaj7   B♭
Be the man I love until the very end.

  C/G   Fmaj7   Am
I've dreamed of you my great love and my best friend.

Outro

C/G F   Em
For God must know how I love you so.

  F   B♭
He's blessed us here today as man and wife.

  C/G   Fmaj7   C
Come dream with me as I've dreamed of you all my life.

G/F F   C/G   F   C
Come dream ____ with me as I have ____ dreamed of you all my life.

In My Life

Words and Music by
John Lennon and Paul McCartney

Melody:

There are   plac - es   I   re - mem-ber...

A   E   F#m   A7/G   D   Dm   G   B

1 2 3   2 3 1   1 3 4 1 1 1   2 1 1 1   1 3 2   2 3 1   2 1   3   1 3 3 3

Intro | A | E | A | E |

                                    A   E   F#m   A7/G
Verse 1   There are places I re-member

                                         D   Dm   A
                         All my life, _____ though some have changed.

                                              E   F#m   A7/G
                         Some forever, not for better,

                                         D   Dm   A
                         Some have gone, _____ and some remain.

                                    F#m   D
Chorus 1   All these places had their moments,

                                 G   A
                         With lovers and friends I still can recall,

                                 F#m   B
                         Some are dead and some are living,

                              Dm   A   E
                         In my life, I've loved them all.

Verse 2
<pre>
                A   E   F#m   A7/G
          But of all these friends and lovers,
                    D Dm   A
          There is no one com-pares with you.
                            E   F#m   A7/G
          And these memories lose their meaning
                    D   Dm   A
          When I think of love as something new.
</pre>

Chorus 2
<pre>
                      F#m   D
          Though I know I'll never lose af-fection
             G   A
          For people and things that went before,
            F#m   B
          I know I'll often stop and think a-bout them.
             Dm   A
          In my life, I love you more.
</pre>

Solo
<pre>
          ‖: A   E |F#m A7/G |D   Dm |A   :‖
</pre>

Chorus 3   *Repeat Chorus 2*

Outro
<pre>
          |A |E |Dm   N.C.   A
                             In my life, I love you more.
          |E |A   ‖
</pre>

The Irish Wedding Song

Words and Music by
Ian Betteridge

Melody:

Here they _ stand,   hand in   hand,

D   A   E7   B7   A7   F7   Bb   Eb   C7   Bb7

Intro | D | A | E7 | A |

Verse 1

E7   A   D   A
Here they stand, hand in hand, they've ex - changed wedding bands.

D   A   B7   E7
To - day is the day of all their dreams and their plans,

A   A7   D   A
And all of their loved ones are here to say

D   A   E7   A
May God bless this couple who marry to - day.

Chorus 1

E7   D   A
In good times and bad times, in sickness and health,

E7   B7   E7
May they know that riches are not needed for wealth.

A   A7   D   A
Help them face problems they'll meet on their way.

D   A   E7   A
May God bless this couple who marry to - day.

| D | A | E7 | A |

Verse 2

E7 A   D   A
May they find peace of mind comes to all who are kind.

   D   A   B7 E7
May the rough times a - head become triumphs in time.

  A A7   D   A
And may their children be happy each day.

   D   A   E7   A
May God bless this fam'ly that started to - day.

Verse 3

F7 B♭   E♭   B♭
As they go, may they know ev'ry love that was shown.

  E♭   B♭   C7   F7
And as life gets shorter, may their feelings grow.

   B♭ B♭7   E♭   B♭
Wher - ever they travel, wher - ever they stay,

   E♭   B♭   F7   B♭
May God bless this couple who marry to - day.

Chorus 2

 F7   E♭   B♭
In good times and bad times, in sickness and health,

 F7   C7   F7
May they know that riches are not needed for wealth.

B♭   B♭7   E♭   B♭
Help them face problems they'll meet on their way.

 E♭   B♭   F7   B♭
May God bless this couple who marry to - day.

   E♭   B♭   F7   E♭ B♭ F7 B♭
Oh, may God bless this couple who married today.

Jesu, Joy of Man's Desiring

English Words by Robert Bridges
Music by Johann Sebastian Bach

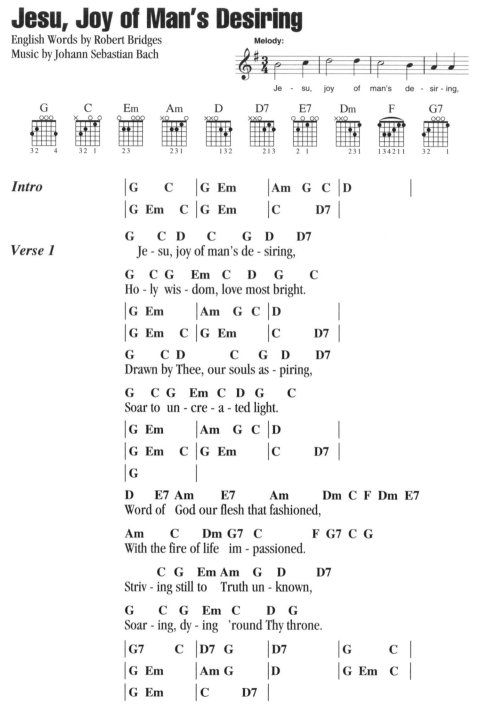

Intro

|G   C |G Em |Am G C |D |
|G Em   C |G Em |C   D7 |

Verse 1

G   C D   C   G D   D7
Je - su, joy of man's de - siring,

G   C G   Em C D G   C
Ho - ly wis - dom, love most bright.

|G Em |Am G C |D |
|G Em   C |G Em |C   D7 |

G   C D   C   G D   D7
Drawn by Thee, our souls as - piring,

G   C G   Em C D G   C
Soar to un - cre - a - ted light.

|G Em |Am G C |D |
|G Em   C |G Em |C   D7 |
|G |

D   E7 Am   E7   Am   Dm C F Dm E7
Word of God our flesh that fashioned,

Am   C   Dm G7 C   F G7 C G
With the fire of life im - passioned.

        C G   Em Am G D   D7
Striv - ing still to Truth un - known,

G   C G   Em C   D G
Soar - ing, dy - ing 'round Thy throne.

G7 C	D7 G	D7	G C
G Em	Am G	D	G Em C
G Em	C D7

Verse 2

```
G      C D       C   G D    D7
Through the way where hope is  guiding,

G   C  G    Em C   D G   C
Hark, what peace - ful  mu - sic rings.

|G Em      |Am  G C |D              |
|G Em   C |G Em       |C      D7 |

G    C D    C   G   D    D7
Where the flock in Thee con - fiding,

G   C G Em C    D   G    C
Drink of joy from death - less springs.

|G Em      |Am  G C |D              |
|G Em   C |G Em       |C      D7 |
|G            |

D    E7 Am    E7   Am    Dm C F Dm E7
Theirs is   beauty's fairest pleasure,

Am      C      Dm G7 C     F G7 C G
Theirs is wisdom's ho - liest treasure.

     C   G Em Am G    C D   D7
Thou dost ev  -  er lead Thine   own,

G C G  Em   C  D G
In the love of    joys un - known.

|G7     C |D7  G    |D7         |G      C |
|G Em      |Am G     |D          |G  Em   C |
|G Em      |C     D7 |G            ‖
```

The Keeper of the Stars

Words and Music by Karen Staley,
Danny Mayo and Dickey Lee

Melody:

It was _ no ac - ci - dent, _

D A13 A/C# Bm G Dadd9/F# Em

A7sus4 A7 A F#m Em* D/F#

Intro

| D | A13 |

Verse 1

D   A/C# Bm   G
It was no accident,   me finding ____ you.

Dadd9/F# Em   A7sus4   A7
Someone had a hand in it   long before we ever ____ knew.

D   A/C#   Bm   G
Now I just can't believe   you're in my ____ life.

Dadd9/F# Em   A7sus4
Heaven's smilin' down on me   as I look at you to - night.

Chorus 1

A7   G   A   F#m
I tip my hat   to the Keeper of the Stars.

G   Em*
He sure knew what He was doin'

A7   D
When He joined these two ____ hearts.

        G   A   F#m
I hold ev'ry - thing   when I hold you in my ____ arms.

G   D/F#   Em*
I've got all ____ I'll ever need,

A7   G   D A13
Thanks to the Keeper of the Stars.

Verse 2

D   A/C♯   Bm   G
Soft moonlight on your face,   oh, how you ___ shine.

             Dadd9/F♯   Em   A7sus4   A7
It takes my ___ breath away   just to look into your ___ eyes.

D   A/C♯   Bm   G
I know I don't deserve   a treasure like ___ you.

             Dadd9/F♯   Em   A7sus4
There really are ___ no words   to show my grati - tude.

Chorus 2

A7   G   A   F♯m
So, I tip my hat   to the Keeper of the Stars.

G   Em*
He sure knew what He was doin'

A7   D
When He joined these two ___ hearts.

           G   A   F♯m
I hold ev'ry - thing   when I hold you in my   arms.

G   D/F♯   Em*
I've got all I'll ever need,

A7   D
Thanks to the Keeper of the Stars.

Outro

D   A/C♯ Bm   G
It was no accident,   me finding ___ you.

             Dadd9/F♯
Someone had a hand in it

Em   A7   D A13 D
Long be - fore we ever knew.

Longer

Words and Music by
Dan Fogelberg

Melody:

Long - er than ___ there've been fish - es in the o-cean,

Open G tuning:
(low to high) D–G–D–G–B–D

G   Am11   Gmaj7/B   Cadd9   G/B   C   Csus2

Bb   Fadd9/C   Ebadd9/Bb   D7sus4/G   D7/F#   Dm7/F

Intro

|G   Am11 |Gmaj7/B   Cadd9 |G   Am11 |

|G/B   C |G   Am11 |G/B   Csus2 |

|Bb   Am11 |G |

Verse 1

G   Am11   Gmaj7/B   Cadd9
Longer than ___ there've been fish - es in the o-cean,

G   Am11 Gmaj7/B   Cadd9
Higher than ___ any bird ever flew,

G   Am11   Gmaj7/B   Cadd9
Longer than ___ there've been stars up in the heav-ens,

Bb   Am11   G
I've been in love ___ with you.

Verse 2

G   Am11 Gmaj7/B   Cadd9
Stronger than ___ any mountain cathe-dral,

G   Am11 Gmaj7/B   Cadd9
Truer than ___ any tree ever grew,

G   Am11 Gmaj7/B   Cadd9
Deeper than ___ any forest prime-val,

Bb   Am11   G
I am in love ___ with you.

Chorus

Fadd9/C   C   E♭add9/B♭   B♭
I'll   bring fire in the win - ters.

Fadd9/C   C   E♭add9/B♭   B♭
You'll   send showers in the springs.

Fadd9/C   C   E♭add9/B♭   B♭
We'll   fly through the falls and summers

      D7sus4/G   D7/F♯   Dm7/F   D7/F♯
With love _____ on our wings.

Verse 3

G   Am11   Gmaj7/B   Cadd9
   Through the years ___ as the fire ___ starts to mellow,

G   Am11   Gmaj7/B   Cadd9
   Burning lines in the book ___ of our lives,

       G   Am11   Gmaj7/B   Cadd9
Though the binding cracks ___ and the pag - es start to yellow,

B♭   Am11   G   B♭   Am11   G
I'll be in love ___ with you.   I'll be in love ___ with you.

Trumpet Solo

‖: Fadd9/C   C | E♭add9/B♭   B♭   :‖ *Play 3 times*
| D7sus4/G   D7/F♯ | Dm7/F   D7/F♯ |

Verse 4

G   Am11   Gmaj7/B   Cadd9
   Longer than ___ there've been fishes in the o - cean,

G   Am11   Gmaj7/B   Cadd9
   Higher than ___ any bird ever flew,

G   Am11   Gmaj7/B   Cadd9
   Longer than ___ there've been stars up in the heav - ens,

B♭   Am11   G   B♭   Am11   G
I've been in love ___ with you.   I am in love ___ with you.

Love Me Tender

from LOVE ME TENDER

Words and Music by
Elvis Presley and Vera Matson

Melody:

Love me _____ ten- der,

D	E7	A7	F#/C#	Bm	D7/A	G	Gm	F#°7	B7
xx0	0 0 00	x0 0 0	x	x	xx0			xx	x
1 3 2	2 1	2 3	3 4 2 1 1	1 3 4 2 1	2 1 3	1 3 4 2 1 1	1 3 4 1 1 1	1 3 2 4 4fr	1 3 1 4 1

Intro |**D** |

Verse 1
> **D**   **E7**
> Love me tender,   love me sweet.
>
> **A7**   **D**
>   Never let me go.
>
>   **E7**
> You have made my life __ complete,
>
> **A7**   **D**
> And I love you so.

Chorus 1
> **D**   **F#/C#**
> Love me tender,
>
> **Bm**   **D7/A**
>   Love me true.
>
> **G**   **Gm**   **D**
> All my dreams ful-fill.
>
>   **F#°7 B7**   **E7**
> For, my   darlin',   I love you,
>
> **A7**   **D**
> And I always will.

Verse 2

D	E7

Love me tender, love me long.

A7   **D**

Take me to your heart.

                 E7

For it's there that I __ belong,

A7   **D**

And we'll never part.

Chorus 2   *Repeat Chorus 1*

Verse 3

D   **E7**

Love me tender,   love me, dear.

A7   **D**

Tell me you are mine.

                   E7

I'll be yours through all __ the years,

A7   **D**

Till the end of time.

Chorus 3

D   **F$\sharp$/C$\sharp$**

Love me tender,

Bm   **D7/A**

  Love me true.

    G   **Gm**   **D**

All __ my dreams ful-fill.

      F$\sharp$°7 **B7**   **E7**

For, my   darling,   I love you,

A7   **D**

And I always will.

Me and You

Words and Music by
Skip Ewing and Ray Herndon

Melody:

Or - di - nar - y? No,   real-ly don't think so,

G   D/F♯   Em7   Bm/D   C   Dsus4   D

C/D   G/B   A7sus4   A7   Am7   D7   B7/D♯

Intro
|G   D/F♯ |Em7 Bm/D |C   Dsus4   D |

Verse 1
G   D/F♯   Em7   Bm/D   C
Ordinar - y? No,   really don't think so,

     G   Dsus4 D
Not a love this true.

G   D/F♯ Em7   Bm/D   C
Common des - tiny,   we were meant to be,

Dsus4   G C/D
Me and you.

Verse 2
G   D/F♯   Em7   Bm/D   C
Like a per - fect scene   from a movie screen,

     G   Dsus4   D
We're a dream come ____ true.

G   D/F♯ Em7   Bm/D C
Suited per - fectly   for e - ternity,

Dsus4   G
Me and you.

Chorus 1

<pre>
C   G/B C/D   G   G/B
Ev'ry day ____ I need you even more,

C   G/B   Dsus4 D
And the night - time, too.

C   G/B   C/D   Em7 A7sus4 A7
There's no way ____ I could ever let you go

Am7   C/D D7
Even if I wanted to.
</pre>

Verse 3

<pre>
G   D/F♯   Em7   Bm/D   C
Ev'ry day ____ I live,   try my best to give

    G   Dsus4 D
All I have to you.

G   D/F♯   Em7   B7/D♯   C
Thank the stars ____ above   that we share this love,

Dsus4   G
Me and you.
</pre>

Guitar Solo   *Repeat Verse 3 (Instrumental)*

Chorus 2   *Repeat Chorus 1*

Verse 4

<pre>
G   D/F♯ Em7   Bm/D   C
Ordinar - y? No,   really don't think so.

    G   Dsus4 D
Just a precious few

G   D/F♯   Em7   B7/D♯ C
Ever make ____ it last,   get as lucky as

Dsus4   G D/F♯ Em7 Bm/D C
Me and you.

Dsus4   D   G
Me and ____ you.
</pre>

More Than Words

Words and Music by
Nuno Bettencourt and Gary Cherone

Melody:

Say-ing "I ___ love ___ you"

G   G/B   Cadd9   Am7   C   D   Dsus4   Em   D7   D/F#

G7   G7/B   Cm   Em7   Bm   D7♭9/A   Dm(add2)/F   Esus4   Csus2   Gm/B♭

Intro ‖: G G/B Cadd9 | Am7 | C | D Dsus4 G   :‖

Verse 1

    G G/B   Cadd9
        Sayin', "I love you"

    Am7   C   D   Dsus4 G
    Is not the words I want to hear from   you.

    G/B   Cadd9   Am7
    It's not that I want you   not to say,

     C   D   Dsus4 Em   Am7 D7
    But if you on - ly   knew how easy it would be,

     G   D/F#   Em
    To show me how you feel.

Chorus 1

              Am7   D7   G7 G7/B C
    More than words is all you have to do to make it real.

            Cm   G   Em
    Then you wouldn't have to say that you love me,

         Am7 D7 G
    'Cause I'd al - ready know.

             D/F#   Em   Bm C
    What would you do___ if my heart was torn in two?

                G/B Am7
    More than words to show you feel

        D7   **G**
That your love for me is real.

           D/F♯   **Em**   **Bm**   **C**
What would you say__ if I took those words a-way?

              G/B **Am7**
Then you couldn't make things new

      D7   **G**
Just by say - in', "I love you."

       G G/B Cadd9   **Am7**
Interlude   La, dee, da , la, dee, da,

         C
Dee, dai, dai, da.

D   **Dsus4 G**   **G/B Cadd9**
More than   words.

           Am7 **D7**
La, dee, da, dai, da.

       G G/B   **Cadd9**   **Am7**
Verse 2   Now that I've tried to   talk to you

      C   **D Dsus4** **G**
And make you un - der - stand,

G/B   **Cadd9**   **Am7**
All you__ have to do is close your eyes

    C   **D Dsus4 Em**
And just reach out your   hands

  Am7   **D7**   **G** **D/F♯ Em**
And__ touch me, hold me close, don't ever let me go.

        Am7   **D7**   **G7**   **G7/B** **C**
Chorus 2   More than words is all I ever needed you__ to show.

      Cm   **G**
Then you wouldn't have to say

      Em
That you love me,

Am7   D   D7♭9/A G
'Cause I'd al - read - y   know.

              D/F♯
What would you do

    Em   Bm   C
If my heart was torn in two?

                 G/B Am7
More than words to show you feel

       D7   G
That your love for me is real.

             D/F♯
What would you say

    Em   Bm   C
If I took those words a-way?

               G/B Am7
Then you couldn't make things new

      D7   G   G/B Cadd9
Just by say - ing "I love   you."

                    Am7
Outro   ‖: La, dee, da, dai, dai,

                C
Dee, dai, dai, da.

D   Dsus4 G   G/B Cadd9
More than   words.   :‖ *Play 3 times*

           Am7
La, dee, da, dai, dai,

            C
Dee, dai, dai, da.

D   Dsus4 G   D/F♯
More than   words.

Dm(add9)/F Esus4
Oo, oo, oo, oo,

          Am7   D
Oo, oo,   oo.

N.C.   G   Csus2 G/B Gm/B♭ Am7 G
More than words.

Nobody Loves Me Like You Do

Words by Pamela Phillips
Music by James P. Dunne

Melody:

Like a can - dle burn - ing bright, __

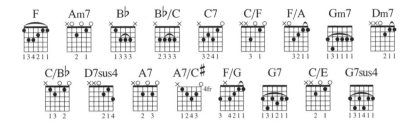

Intro ‖: F   Am7 │Bb Bb/C C7 :‖

Verse 1

                    F   C/F   Bb   F/A
Female: Like a candle burn - ing bright,

Gm7   C7   Am7
Love is glowing in your eyes.

Dm7 Bb   C/Bb
A flame to light our way,

       Am7   D7sus4 Dm7
That burns ____ brighter ev'ry day.

Bb   A7 A7/C# Dm7 F/G G7
Now I have _____ you,

Gm7 F/A   Bb   C7   F   Am7 Bb Bb/C C7
No - body loves ____ me   like you do.

Verse 2   *Male:*

      F   C/F   Bb   F/A
Like a leaf upon ___ the wind,

Gm7   C7   Am7
I could find ___ no place ___ to land.

Dm7 Bb   C/Bb
I dreamed the hours a - way,

   Am7   D7sus4 Dm7
And wondered ev'ry day,

   Bb   A7 A7/C# Dm7 F/G G7
Do ___ dreams come ____ true?

Gm7 F/A   Bb   C7   F   C/E
No - body loves ___ me   like you do.

Chorus 1   *Both:*

    Bb   Am7
What if I never met ___ you?

Bb   Am7
Where would I be right now?

Bb   A7   A7/C#   Dm7 G7sus4 G7
Funny how life just falls ___ in place ___ some - how.

     Bb   F/A
Male: You touched my heart in places

      Gm7   F/A
Female: That I never even knew.

   Gm7 F/A   Bb   C7   F   Am7 Bb Bb/C C7
Both: No - body loves ___ me ___ like you ___ do.

Verse 3

        F   C/F   Bb   F/A
Male: I was words without ____ a tune.

        Gm7   C7   Am7
Female: I was a song ____ still un - sung.

      Dm7 Bb   C/Bb
Male: A poem with no rhyme,

        Am7   D7sus4 Dm7
Female: A dancer out of time.

        Bb   A7 A7/C#   Dm7 F/G G7
Both: But now there's _____ you.

Gm7 F/A   Bb   C7   F   C/E
No - body loves ___ me ___ like you ___ do.

Chorus 2

        Bb   Am7
Both: What if I never met ___ you?

Bb   Am7
Where would I be right now?

Bb   A7   A7/C#   Dm7 G7sus4 G7
Funny how life just falls ___ in place ___ some - how.

        Bb   F/A
Female: You touched my heart in places

        Gm7   F/A
Male: That I never even knew.

     Gm7 F/A   Bb   Gm7 F/A   Bb
Both: No - body loves ___ me, no - body loves ___ me.

Gm7 F/A   Bb   A7/C#   Dm7   G7sus4 G7
No - body loves ___ me ___ like you ___ do.

Gm7 F/A   Bb/C   F Am7 Bb Bb/C C7 F
No - body loves ___ me like you do.

My Heart Will Go On

(Love Theme from 'Titanic')

from the Paramount and Twentieth Century Fox Motion Picture TITANIC

Music by James Horner
Lyric by Will Jennings

Melody:

Ev - 'ry night in   my dreams

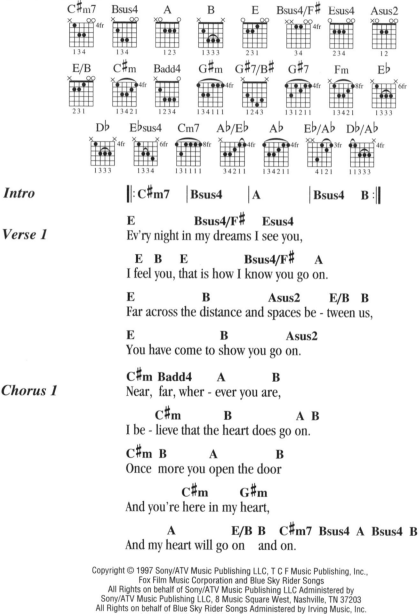

C#m7 Bsus4 A B E Bsus4/F# Esus4 Asus2

E/B C#m Badd4 G#m G#7/B# G#7 Fm Eb

Db Ebsus4 Cm7 Ab/Eb Ab Eb/Ab Db/Ab

Intro
‖: C#m7 | Bsus4 | A | Bsus4 B :‖

Verse 1

  E   Bsus4/F# Esus4
Ev'ry night in my dreams I see you,

    E B E   Bsus4/F# A
I feel you, that is how I know you go on.

  E   B   Asus2   E/B B
Far across the distance and spaces be - tween us,

  E   B   Asus2
You have come to show you go on.

Chorus 1

 C#m Badd4   A   B
Near, far, wher - ever you are,

     C#m   B   A B
I be - lieve that the heart does go on.

 C#m B   A   B
Once more you open the door

        C#m   G#m
And you're here in my heart,

      A   E/B B C#m7 Bsus4 A Bsus4 B
And my heart will go on   and on.

Verse 2

E   B   Asus2 E/B B
Love can touch us one time and last for a life - time,

E   B   Asus2
And never let go till we're gone.

E   B   Asus2   E/B G#7/B#
Love was when I loved you, one true time I'd hold to.

C#m   G#m   Asus2
In my life we'll always go on.

Chorus 2

C#m Badd4 A   B
Near, far, wher - ever you are,

     C#m   B   A B
I believe ____ that the heart does go on.

C#m B   A   B
Once more you open the door

      C#m   G#m
And you're here in my heart,

     A   E/B B C#m7 Bsus4 A Bsus4 B
And my heart will go on and on.

| C#m7 | Bsus4 | A | C#m G#7 | |

Outro-Chorus

Fm Eb   Db   Eb
You're here, there's nothing I fear

     Fm   Eb   Db Ebsus4 Eb
And I know ____ that my heart ____ will go on.

Fm Eb   Db   Eb
We'll stay for - ever this way.

     Fm   Cm7
You are safe ____ in my heart,

    Db   Ab/Eb Eb Ab Eb/Ab Db/Ab
And my heart will go on and on.

Eb/Ab Ab Eb/Ab Db/Ab Ab
 Mm.

Now and Forever
(You and Me)

Words and Music by Jim Vallance,
Randy Goodrum and David Foster

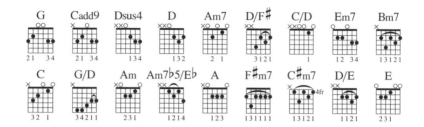

Intro

‖: G | Cadd9 | Dsus4 | D :‖

Verse 1

    G   **Cadd9**   **Dsus4 D**
Up until now I've learned to live without love,

       G   **Cadd9**   **Dsus4 D**
Like a ship without a sail, wan - dering aimlessly lost.

      Am7   **D/F♯**
I never knew how it felt to lose my control,

          Am7   **C/D D**
But now that I've found you, this is all so new.

Chorus 1

    G   **Em7**
You and me, we've got a destiny.

        Bm7 C   **G/D D**
Starting tonight, ____ we'll be to - geth - er.

    G   **Em7**
You and me, this is what love should be,

          Bm7 C/D   **G Cadd9 Dsus4 D**
And it's gonna be right, ____ now and forev - er.

	G Cadd9 Dsus4 D
Verse 2	Darlin', inside your eyes, I can see mysteries there.

       G   Cadd9   Dsus4 D
And you're melting the ice sur - rounding me, I'm no longer scared.

     Am7   D/F♯
I feel you inside my soul, and I'm captured tonight.

      Am7   C/D D
But don't let go, this is para - dise.

	G Em7
Chorus 2	You and me, we've got a destiny.

         Bm7 C   G/D D
Starting tonight, ____ we'll be to - geth - er.

    G   Em7
You and me, this is what love should be,

          Bm7
And it's gonna be right.

	Am
Bridge	If you tell me there's a heaven up above,

    Am7♭5/E♭
Then that's what I'll believe,

'Cause you're the one thing that I'm so sure of.

Guitar Solo	*Repeat Intro*

	Am7 D/F♯
Verse 3	I feel you inside my soul, and I'm captured tonight.

      Am7   C/D D
But don't let go, this is para - dise.

	A F♯m7
Chorus 3	‖: You and me, we've got a destiny.

        C♯m7 D/E   D/F♯ E
Starting tonight, _____ we'll be to - geth - er.

    A   F♯m7
You and me, this is what love should be,

        C♯m7 D/E   D/F♯ E
And it's gonna be right, _____ now and for - ev - er. :‖ *Repeat*
                                    and fade

Ode to Joy
from SYMPHONY NO. 9 IN D MINOR, FOURTH MOVEMENT CHORAL THEME

Words by Henry van Dyke
Music by Ludwig van Beethoven

Melody:

Joy - ful, joy - ful   we   a - dore Thee,

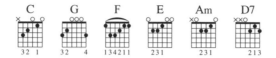

C   G   F   E   Am   D7

Verse 1

    C   G
Joyful, joyful we adore Thee,

    C   G
God of glory, Lord of love.

    C   F
Hearts unfold like flowers before Thee,

    C   G   C
Op'ning to the sun a - bove.

    G   C   G   C
Melt the clouds of sin and sadness,

    G   E   Am D7 G
Drive the dark of doubt a - way.

    C   F
Giver of im - mortal gladness,

    C   G   C
Fill us with the light of day.

Verse 2

C   G
Mortals, join the happy chorus

C   G
Which the morning stars be - gan.

C   F
Father love is reigning o'er us,

C   G   C
Brother love bonds man to man.

G C   G   C
Ever singing, march we onward,

G   E   Am D7 G
Victors in the midst of   strife.

C   F
Joyful music leads us onward

C   G   C
In the triumph song of life.

One in a Million You

Words and Music by
Sam Dees

Melody:

Love had played _ its games _ on me _ so long _

(Capo 1st fret)

D/E   Amaj7   A   A7   G/B   A7/C#   Dmaj7   G13   G7   A/E

Bm7   Esus4   F°7   F#m7   C#m7   A7/G   D   E   Aadd9

Intro ‖: D/E | |Amaj7 | :‖

Verse 1
    A   **Amaj7**
Love had played its games on me so long

            A7   **G/B**   **A7/C#** **Dmaj7**
I started to ____ believe I'd never find _____ anyone.

             G13   **G7**   **A/E**
Doubt had tried ____ to convince ____ me to give in,

            Bm7
Said, "You can't win."

Verse 2
  Esus4   **A**   **Amaj7**
 But one day the sun came a shinin' through.

         A7   **G/B**   **A7/C#**   **Dmaj7**   **G13**
The rain ____ had stopped   and the skies ____ were ____ blue,

        G7   **A/E**   **F°7** **F#m7**
And, oh, ____ what a revela - tion to   see

         Bm7   **D/E**
Some - one was saying "I love you" to me.

Chorus 1

    A   Amaj7 A7   G/B A7/C♯ Dmaj7
A one in a mil - lion, chance ___ of a life - time.

      G13 G7   A/E
And life ___ showed com - passion

       Bm7 C♯m7 Dmaj7 Esus4   A
And sent to me a   stroke of love called you,

A7/G   D G13
  A one in a million you.

Verse 3

G7   A   Amaj7
  I was a lonely man with empty arms to fill,

     A7   G/B   A7/C♯ Dmaj7
Then I found a piece of happiness ___ to call my own.

    G13   G7   A/E
And life is worth living a - gain,

      Bm7   D/E
For to love ___ you, to me, is to live.

Chorus 2

    A   Amaj7 A7   G/B A7/C♯ Dmaj7
A one in a mil - lion, chance ___ of a life - time.

      G13 G7   A/E
And life ___ showed com - passion

       Bm7 C♯m7 Dmaj7 Esus4   A
And sent to me a   stroke of love called you,

A7/G   D Esus4 E
  A one in a million you.

Chorus 3

    A   Amaj7 A7   G/B A7/C♯ Dmaj7
A one in a million, chance ___ of a   lifetime.

      G13 G7   A/E
And life ___ showed com - passion

       Bm7 C♯m7 Dmaj7 Esus4   A
And sent to me a   stroke of love called you,

A7/G   D
  A one in a million you.

G13   G7   Aadd9
  A one ___ in a million you.

Sunrise, Sunset

Words by Sheldon Harnick
Music by Jerry Bock

Melody:

Is this the lit - tle girl I

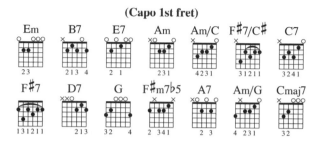

(Capo 1st fret)

Em B7 E7 Am Am/C F#7/C# C7

F#7 D7 G F#m7b5 A7 Am/G Cmaj7

Intro ‖: Em | :‖

Verse 1

     Em   B7   Em
Male: Is this the little girl I carried?

       B7   Em E7
Is this the little boy at play?

       Am   E7   Am Am/C
Female: I don't re - member growing old - er.

F#7/C# C7 B7
When did they?

Verse 2

      Em   B7   Em
Male: When did she get to be a beauty?

      B7   Em E7
When did he grow to be this tall?

      Am   E7   Am F#7 B7
Female: Wasn't it yesterday when they were small?

Chorus 1

Em   Am Em B7
Male: Sun - rise, sun - set.

Em   Am Em B7
Sun - rise, sun - set.

Em   Am Em Am Em E7
Swift - ly   flow the days.

Am   D7   G
Seedlings turn overnight to sunflowers

F#m7b5 B7   Em
Blossoming even as we gaze.

Chorus 2

Em   Am Em B7
Female: Sun - rise, sun - set.

Em   Am Em B7
Sun - rise, sun - set.

Em   Am Em Am Em E7
Swift - ly   fly the years.

F#m7b5 B7   Em A7
One season following an - oth - er

F#m7b5 B7   Em
Laden with happiness and tears.

Verse 3

Em   B7   Em
Male: What words of wisdom can I give them?

B7   Em E7
How can I help to ease their way?

Am   E7   Am Am/G
Female: Now they must learn from one an - oth - er

F#7 B7
Day by day.

Verse 4

      Em   B7   Em
Male: They look so natural to - gether.

                   B7   Em E7
Female: Just like two newlyweds should be.

      Am   E7   Am F♯7 B7
Both: Is there a canopy in store for   me?

Chorus 3

      Em   Am Em B7
Both: Sun - rise, sun - set.

Em   Am Em B7
Sun - rise, sun - set.

Em   Am Em Am Em E7
Swift - ly   flow the days.

Am   D7   G   Cmaj7
Seedlings turn overnight to sun - flowers

F♯m7♭5 B7   Em
Blossoming even as we gaze.

Chorus 4

      Em   Am Em B7
Both: Sun - rise, sun - set.

Em   Am Em B7
Sun - rise, sun - set.

Em   Am Em Am Em E7
Swift - ly   fly the   years.

F♯m7♭5 B7   Em A7
One season following an - oth - er

F♯m7♭5 B7   N.C. Em
Laden with happiness and tears.

This I Swear

Words and Music by
John Reid and David Erikkson

Melody:

You're there by my __ side _____

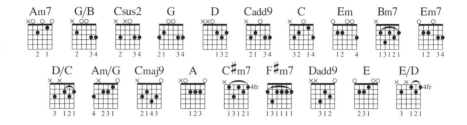

Intro | Am7 G/B | Csus2 |

Verse 1

G   D   Cadd9
You're there by my side ____ in every way.

Am7   D   G
I know that you will not ____ forsake me.

                         D   C
I give you my life, ____ I would not think twice.

         D
Your love is all I need, believe me.

Pre-Chorus 1

Em   C   G   D
I may not say it quite as much as I should

Em   C   G   D
But when I say I love you, darling, that means for good.

Am7   Bm7   Cadd9
So open up your heart ____ and let me in.

Chorus 1

               G   Bm7
And I will love you till forev - er.

        Em7   Cadd9
Until death do us part, we'll be to - gether.

            G   D
So, take my hand and hold on tight,

      C D/C C   D   G   Am/G
And we'll get   there.   This I swear.

Verse 2

G   D   Cadd9
  I'm wondering how ____ I ever got by

      Am7   D   G
With - out you in my life ____ to guide me.

            D   C
Wherever I go, ____ the one thing that's true,

      D
Is ev'rything I do, I do for you.

Pre-Chorus 2

  Em   C   G   D
  I may not say it half as much as I should

Em   C   G   D
  But when I say I love you, darling, that means for good.

  Am7   Bm7   Cadd9
So open up your heart ____ and let me in.

Chorus 2

               G   Bm7
And I will love you till forev - er.

        Em7   Cadd9
Until death do us part, we'll be to - gether.

            G   D
So, take my hand and hold on tight,

      C D/C C   D   G
And we'll get   there.   This I swear.

Bridge

    D   C   G   D
So when - ever you get weary, just reach out for me.

    C   Am7 G/B   Cmaj9
I'll never let you down,   my love.

Chorus 3

N.C.   A   C#m7
And I will love you until ___ forever.

    F#m7   Dadd9
Until death do us part, we'll be to - gether.

        A   E
So, take my hand and hold on tight,

        D   E/D D
And we'll get   there.

Outro-Chorus

    E   A   C#m7
And I will love you until forev - er.

    F#m7   Dadd9
Until death do us part, we'll be to - gether.

        A   E
So, take my hand and hold on tight,

        D   E/D   D
And we'll get there.   Oh, ___ we'll get there.

E   A
And this I ___ swear.

This Is the Day
(A Wedding Song)

Words and Music by
Scott Wesley Brown

Melody:

This   is   the   day ___   that the   Lord ___

E5   F#5/E   E   G#m7   Asus2   C#m7

F#m7add4   B7(no3rd)   Asus2*   F#m7   B7   E*

Intro

‖: E5 F#5/E │E5 F#5/E :‖

Verse 1

    E   G#m7   Asus2   E
This is the day ___ that the Lord ___ hath made,

    C#m7   G#m7   F#m7add4 B7(no3rd)
And I'm so glad ___ He made ___ you.

      E   G#m7   Asus2   E
With each rising sun ___ you are here by my side,

    C#m7   G#m7   F#m7add4
You are more than a dream ___ come true.

B7(no3rd) C#m7   G#m7
Oh, to   have you, to hold ___ you,

    F#m7add4   B7(no3rd)
To love you, to pray.

    C#m7   G#m7
To share with, to care ___ with,

    F#m7add4   B7(no3rd)
To hold hands and say

E   G#m7   Asus2*   E
This is the day ___ that the Lord hath made,

    Asus2*   E C#m7   G#m7
And I will rejoice, ___ I will rejoice,

F#m7   B7   E5 F#5/E E5 F#5/E
I will rejoice ___ with you.

│E5 F#5/E │E5 F#5/E │

Verse 2

E   G#m7   Asus2   E
This is the love ____ that the Lord ____ hath made,

    C#m7   G#m7   F#m7add4 B7(no3rd)
That you and I ____ are one.

E   G#m7   Asus2   E
Love's mystery ____ is un - folding to - day,

C#m7   G#m7   F#m7add4
Written for us in the Son.

B7(no3rd) C#m7   G#m7   F#m7add4 B7(no3rd)
Oh, for   better, for worse, for rich or for   poor,

C#m7   G#m7 F#m7add4 B7(no3rd)
  Each day that pass - es   I'll love you more,

      E   G#m7   Asus2*   E
'Cause this is the day that the Lord hath made,

    Asus2*   E C#m7   G#m7
And I will rejoice, ____ I will rejoice,

F#m7   B7   E5 F#5/E
I will rejoice ____ with you.

Outro

E*   C#m7 G#m7 F#m7add4
  This is the day.

B7(no3rd)   C#m7 G#m7 Asus2*
  This is the day.

B7(no3rd)   C#m7 G#m7 F#m7add4
  This is the day.

B7(no3rd)   C#m7 G#m7 Asus2*
  This is the day.

|E5 F#5/E |E5 F#5/E |E5 F#5/E |E*   ‖

Through the Years

Words and Music by
Steve Dorff and Marty Panzer

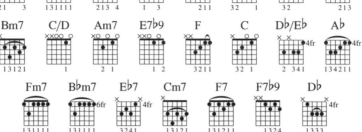

Verse 1

      G   **F#m7**   **B7**   **Em7**
I can't remember when__ you were - n't there,

Dm7 **G7**   **Cmaj7** **D7**   **Bm7** **C/D**
When I didn't care__ for anyone but you,

     G   **F#m7**   **B7**   **Em7**
I swear we've been through ev'rything __ there is,

         Dm7   **G7**   **Cmaj7**
Can't imagine anything ____ we've missed.

       G   **Am7**   **C/D**
Can't imagine anything the two of us can't do.

Chorus 1

          G
Through the years

     Em7   **Am7**
You've never let me down,

      C/D   **D7 Bm7**
You've turned my life__ a - round.

     Em7   **Am7**
The sweetest days I've found

          C/D
I've found with you.

D7   **Bm7**
Through the years,

     E7♭9   **Am7**
I've never been a-fraid,

     D7   **Bm7**
I've loved the life we've made,

     E7♭9   **Cmaj7**
And I'm so glad I've stayed

       Bm7   **Am7**
Right here with you

C/D   **G**   **Em7**   **F C C/D**
Through the years.

Verse 2

   G   **F♯m7**   **B7**   **Em7**
I can't remember what__ I used__ to do,

Dm7 G7   **Cmaj7**
Who I trusted, who

 D7   **Bm7**
I listened to be-fore.

   G   **F♯m7**   **B7**   **Em7**
I swear you've taught me ev'rything __ I know,

       Dm7   **G7**   **Cmaj7**
Can't imagine needing some - one so.

            G
But through the years it seems to me

 Am7   **C/D**
I need you more and more.

Chorus 2

               G
Through the years,

        Em7   **Am7**
Through all the good and bad,

C/D   **D7** **Bm7**
I knew how much__ we__ had.

    Em7   **Am7**   **C/D**
I've always been so glad to be with you.

D7   **Bm7**
Through the years,

   E7b9   **Am7**
It's better ev'ry day.

      D7   **Bm7**
You've kissed my tears a-way.

    E7b9   **Cmaj7**
As long as it's o-kay

     Bm7   **Am7**
I'll stay with you

C/D   **G**   **Db/Eb**
Through the years.

Chorus 3

            Ab
Through the years

     Fm7   **Bbm7**
When ev - 'rything went wrong,

 Db/Eb Eb7   **Cm7**
To-gether we were strong.

  F7   **Bbm7**
I know that I belonged

           Db/Eb
Right here with you.

Eb7   **Cm7**
Through the years

 F7b9   **Bbm7**
I never had a doubt

     Eb7   **Cm7**
We'd al - ways work things out.

   F7b9   **Db**
I've learned what love's about

   Cm7 **Bbm7**
By loving you

Db/Eb   **Ab**
Through the years.

Chorus 4

         A♭
Through the years

    Fm7   **B♭m7**
You've never let me down,

    D♭/E♭   **E♭7** **Cm7**
You've turned my life__ a - round.

    F7   **B♭m7**
The sweetest days I've found

          D♭/E♭
I've found with you.

E♭7   **Cm7**
Through the years,

   F7♭9
It's better ev'ry day;

     E♭7   **Cm7**
You've kissed my tears a-way.

   F7♭9   **D♭**
As long as it's okay

   Cm7   **B♭m7**
I'll stay with you

D♭/E♭   **A♭**
Through the years.

Tonight, I Celebrate My Love

Music by Michael Masser
Lyric by Gerry Goffin

Melody:

To - night   I cel - e - brate my love _____ for you. _

(Capo 1st fret)

D   G   A   Bm7   Em7   G/A   F#m7

Gmaj7   A/D   G/D   C/D   D7   Gm(maj7)

Intro
| D | G   A |

Verse 1
>   D   G   A
> *Female:* To - night I celebrate my love for you.

>   D   G   A
> It seems the natural thing to do.

>   D   Bm7   Em7
> *Male:* To - night no one's gonna find ____ us,

>   G/A   G   F#m7
> We'll leave the world be - hind us,

>   Bm7   Em7
> *Both:*   When I make love to you.

Verse 2
>   G/A   A   D   G   A
> *Female:*   To - night I celebrate my love for you

>   D   G   A
> And hope that deep inside you feel it too.

>   D   Bm7   Em7
> *Male:* To - night our spirits will be climb - ing

>   G/A   G   F#m7
> To a sky lit up ____ with diamonds

>   Bm7   Gmaj7   G/A   D   A/D   G/D
> *Both:*   When I make love to you   to - night.

Chorus 1 *Both:* To - night I celebrate my love for you
                Gmaj7   **F♯m7**

    C/D **D7**   **Gmaj7**   **F♯m7**
      And that midnight sun is gonna come shining through.

        C/D **D7**   **Gmaj7** **F♯m7** **Em7**   **F♯m7**
Male: To - night _____   they'll be no distance be - tween us.

      Bm7   **Gmaj7**   **Gm(maj7)**   **D**   **G A**
Female: What I want most to do is to get close to you *Both:* to - night.

Verse 3 *Female:* To - night I celebrate my love for you
               D   **G**   **A**

      D   **G**   **A**
    And soon this old world will seem brand - new.

         D **Bm7**   **Em7**
Male: To - night we will both dis - cover

     G/A   **G** **F♯m7**
How friends turn into lovers,

     Bm7   **Gmaj7**   **G/A A**
Both: When I make love to you.

Chorus 2 *Both:* To - night I celebrate my love for you
                Gmaj7   **F♯m7**

    C/D **D7**   **Gmaj7**   **F♯m7**
      And that midnight sun is gonna come shining through.

        C/D **D7**   **Gmaj7** **F♯m7** **Em7**   **F♯m7**
Male: To - night _____   they'll be no distance be - tween us.

      Bm7   **Gmaj7**   **Gm(maj7)**
Female: What I want most to do is to get close to you.

      D   **G**   **A** **G/A**   **D**
Both: To - night I celebrate my love for you, ____ to - night.

True Love
from HIGH SOCIETY

Words and Music by
Cole Porter

Melody:

While I give to you ___ and you ___ give ___

(Capo 1st fret)

D G G#°7 A7 A7/G G/D Gm7 C7

F D7sus2 D+ F7 Bm6 G/A C#m7♭5

		D	G		G#°7 D

Verse *Male:* While I give to you and you give to me,

A7 A7/G G/D D
True love, true love.

G G#°7 D
So on and on it'll always be,

A7 A7/G G/D D
True love, true love.

Gm7 C7 F D7sus2 D+
Chorus 1 *Male:* For you and I have a guardian an - gel

Gm7 C7 F7
On high with nothing to do.

A7 D G G#°7 D
But to give to you and to give to me,

A7 D
Love forever true.

Gm7 C7 F D7sus2 D+
Chorus 2 *Male/Female:* For you and I have a guardian an - gel

Gm7 C7 F7
On high with nothing to do.

A7 D G G#°7 D
But to give to you and to give to me,

A7 D A7 D Bm6 G/A C#m7♭5 D
Love forever true. Love forever true.

You'll Accomp'ny Me

Words and Music by
Bob Seger

Melody:

A gyp-sy wind is blow-ing   warm _ to - night. _

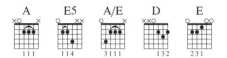

Intro   ‖: A   E5 | A/E   E5   :‖   *Play 4 times*

| | A   E5   A/E   E5
Verse 1 | A gyp - sy wind is blowing warm to - night.

              | A   E5   A/E   E5
              | The sky is starlit and the time is right.

              | A   E5   A/E   E5
              | And still you're tellin' me you have ____ to go.

              | A   E5   A/E   E5
              | Before you leave, there's something you should know.

              | A E5   A/E   E5   A   E5 A/E E5
              | Yeah,   something you should know, ____ babe.

              | A   E5   A/E   E5
Verse 2 | I've seen you smiling in the sum - mer sun.

              | A   E5   A/E   E5
              | I've seen your long hair flying when you run.

              | A   E5   A/E   E5
              | I've made my mind up that it's meant to be.

              | A   E5   A/E   E5
              | Some - day, lady, you'll ac - comp'ny me.

Chorus 1
      A   D   A
      Someday, lady, you'll ac - comp'ny me

                                         E
  Out where the rivers meet the sounding sea.

  A   D   A
    You're high above me, now, you're wild ___ and free,

          A   E5   A/E   E5
  Ah, but   some - day, lady, you'll ac - comp'ny me.

  A   E5   A/E   E5
  Some - day, lady, you'll ac - comp'ny me, yeah.

Interlude
  |A   E5 |A/E E5 |A   E5 |A/E E5 |
    Oo.

Verse 3
  A   E5   A/E E5
  Some peo - ple say that love's a losin' game.

  A   E5   A/E   E5
  You start with fire, but you lose the flame.

  A   E5   A/E   E5
  The ashes ___ smolder, but the warmth's ___ soon gone.

  A   E5   A/E E5
  You end up cold and lonely on your own.

  A   E5   A/E E5
  I'll take my chances, babe, I'll risk it all.

  A   E5   A/E   E5
  I'll win your love, or I'll take the fall.

  A   E5   A/E   E5
  I made my mind up, girl, it's meant to be.

  A   E5   A/E   E5
  Some - day, lady, you'll ac - comp'ny me.

Chorus 2

A   D   A
Someday, lady, you'll ac - comp'ny me.

                                             E
It's written down somewhere, it's got to be.

A   D   A
You're high above me flyin' wild and free,

          E5   A/E   E5
Oh, but some - day, lady, you'll ac - comp'ny me.

A   E5   A/E   E5
Some - day, lady, you'll ac - comp'ny me.

Chorus 3

A   D   A
Someday, lady, you'll ac - comp'ny me

                                    E
Out where the rivers meet the sounding sea.

A   D   A
I feel it in my soul, it's meant to be.

          E5   A/E   E5
Oh, some - day, lady, you'll ac - comp'ny me.

A   E5   A/E   E5
Some - day, lady, you'll ac - comp'ny me.

You will accomp'ny me.

Outro

    A   E5 A/E E5
‖: (Oo, hoo,)

  A   E5   A/E   E5
(Oo, hoo, you'll ac - comp'ny me.) :‖ *Repeat and fade*
                                            w/ lead vocal ad lib.

Truly

Words and Music by
Lionel Richie

(Capo 1st fret)

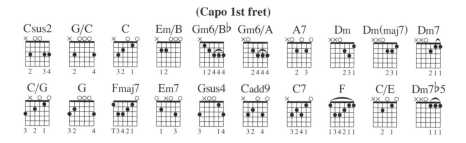

Intro	|Csus2 G/C |Csus2 G/C |	

Verse 1

    C   **Em/B**   **Gm6/B♭ Gm6/A A7**
Girl, tell me only this, that I have your heart for always,

      Dm   **Dm(maj7)**   **Dm7**
And ___ you want me by your side whispering the words

          C/G G
"I'll always love you."

Pre-Chorus 1

           Fmaj7 Em7   **Fmaj7**
And forev - er,   I will be your ___ lover,

  Em7   **Fmaj7**   **Em7**
  And I know if you really care,

      Dm7   **Gsus4**   **G Gsus4 G**
I will always be ___ there.

GUITAR CHORD SONGBOOK

Verse 2
              C   **Em/B**
Now, I need to tell you this,

                    Gm6/B♭ Gm6/A A7
There's no other love like   your love.

       Dm   **Dm(maj7)**
And I, as long as I live,

              Dm7   **C/G**   **G**
I'll give you all the joy my heart and soul can give.

Pre-Chorus 2
        Fmaj7 Em7   **Fmaj7**
Let me hold you.   I need to have you   near me,

Em7   **Fmaj7** **Em7**
 And I feel, with you in my ___ arms,

   Dm7   **Gsus4 G**
This love will last forev   er.

Chorus
        Gsus4 G Cadd9 C7   **Fmaj7**   **Gsus4**
Be - cause   I'm truly, _____ truly in love with you, girl.

   Cadd9 C7   **Fmaj7**   **Gsus4**
I'm truly, _____ head o - ver heels with your love.

   Cadd9   **C7**   **Fmaj7**   **Gsus4**
I need you, ___ and with your love I'm free.

   Cadd9 C7   **F**   **C/E** **Dm7 Dm7♭5 Cadd9**
And truly, _____ you know you're all right ____ with   me.

We've Only Just Begun

Words and Music by
Roger Nichols and Paul Williams

Melody:

We've on - ly just be-gun ___

A   Dmaj7   C#m7   F#m7   Bm7   E7sus4   E7

Amaj7   E   F#   Bmaj7   Bb   Ebmaj7   C#

Intro
| A | Dmaj7 | A | Dmaj7 |

Verse 1

A   Dmaj7 C#m7
We've only just be - gun   to live,

F#m7   Bm7
White lace and ___ promises,

F#m7   Bm7   E7sus4 E7
A kiss for luck and we're on our way.

Verse 2

A   Dmaj7 C#m7
Before the rising sun we _____ fly.

F#m7   Bm7
So many roads to choose,

F#m7   Bm7   E7sus4
We start out walking and learn to run.

                        Amaj7 Dmaj7 Amaj7 Dmaj7 E
(And, yes, we've just be - gun.)

Bridge 1

F#   Bmaj7   F#   Bmaj7
Sharing ho - rizons that are new to us,

F#   Bmaj7   F# Bmaj7
Watching the signs ___ along the way.

Bb   Ebmaj7   Bb   Ebmaj7
Talking it over, just the two of us,

Bb   Ebmaj7   E7sus4 E7
Working to - gether day to day, to - gether.

Verse 3

    A   Dmaj7   C#m7
And when the evening comes we smile,

F#m7   Bm7
So much of life ahead,

F#m7   Bm7   E7sus4
We'll find a place where there's room to grow.

                               Amaj7 Dmaj7 Amaj7 Dmaj7 E
(And, yes, we've just be - gun.)

Bridge 2

F#   Bmaj7   F#   Bmaj7
Sharing ho - rizons that are new to us,

F#   Bmaj7   F# Bmaj7
Watching the signs ___ along the way.

Bb   Ebmaj7   Bb   Ebmaj7
Talking it over, just the two of us,

Bb   Ebmaj7   E7sus4 E7   NC.
Working to - gether day to day, to - gether, together.

Verse 4

    A   Dmaj7   C#m7
And when the evening comes we smile,

F#m7   Bm7
So much of life ahead,

F#m7   Bm7   E7sus4
We'll find a place where there's room to grow.

                               Amaj7 Dmaj7 Amaj7 Dmaj7 C#
And, yes, we've just be - gun.

Wedding Prayer

Words and Music by
Mary Rice Hopkins

Melody:

Lord, ___ take our lives ___

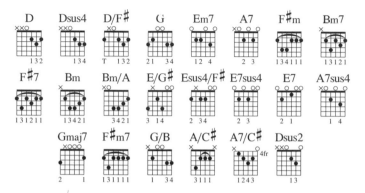

Intro | D   Dsus4 | D   Dsus4 |

Verse 1
D   D/F# G
Lord, take our lives

D/F# Em7   A7   D
  As two who love You ___ join as one.

   F#m   Bm7
And let our love grow as Your love___ grows in us.

F#m   F#7
Bind us togeth - er

     Bm   Bm/A   E/G#   Esus4/F#   E7sus4
So we learn how to trust ___ in You.

E7   A7sus4 A7
   Trust in You.

Verse 2

D　　　　D/F♯　G　D/F♯
Father, You are love

Em7　　　　　A7　　　　　D
From the begin - ning of time.

　F♯m　　　　　　Bm7
You made us to join as man and wife,

F♯m　　　F♯7　　　　　　Bm　　Bm/A
To live to - gether, the Cre - ator of life,

　　　　　　E/G♯　Esus4/F♯　E7sus4　E7　　　　　A7sus4　A7
We love You, _____ we love You.

Bridge

Gmaj7　　　　F♯m7　　　　　Em7　A7　　　　D
Our prayer is ___ that our love　　　grows in You.

　　　　　Em7　　　　A7　　　　　Em7　　　　A7
'Cause You've blessed our lives, and You saved us in - side,

　　　Em7　　　　　　　　　A7sus4　A7
Now, to - gether we want to serve You.

Verse 3

G/B　A/C♯　D　　D/F♯　　　　　G　D/F♯
So,　Lord, ___ use our lives

Em7　　　A7　　　　　D
As we jour - ney from here.

　F♯m　　　　　　　　Bm7
And make our love strong, yet gentle and true,

　F♯m　　　　F♯7　　　　Bm　　Bm/A
In all that we are ___ let us glor - ify You.

　　　　　E/G♯　Esus4/F♯　E7sus4　E7　　　　　A7sus4　A7
Ooh, ooh, ooh. _____　Ooh, ooh, ooh.

　　　　　D　D/F♯　G　D/F♯
Ooh, ooh, ooh.

Em7　A7　　　　A7/C♯　D　Dsus4　D　Dsus2　D
Ooh,　ooh, ooh, ooh,　ooh.

Wedding Song
(There Is Love)

Words and Music by
Paul Stookey

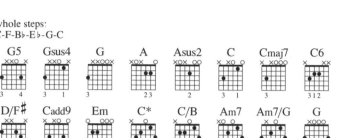

Melody:

He is now to be a - mong you

Tune down 2 whole steps:
(low to high) C-F-Bb-Eb-G-C

G5   Gsus4   G   A   Asus2   C   Cmaj7   C6

D/F#   Cadd9   Em   C*   C/B   Am7   Am7/G   G

Intro

G5				
	Gsus4	G	A Asus2|	
C Cmaj7 C6	C	G5 Gsus4 G	Gsus4

Verse 1

         G5   D/F#
He is now to be among you at the calling of your hearts.

Cadd9   **G5**
Rest assured, this troubadour is acting on His part.

                 D/F#   **Cadd9**   **G5**
The union of your spirits here has caused Him to remain,

          Em   **G5**   **D/F#**
For when - ever two or more of you are gathered in His name

        Cadd9   **G5**   **Gsus4 G A Asus2**
There is love, there is ___ love.

|C Cmaj7 C6| C | G5 Gsus4 G |

Verse 2

Gsus4 G5   D/F#   Cadd9   G5
Well, a man shall leave his mother, and a woman leave her home.

Em   G5   D/F#
They shall travel on to where the two shall be as one.

     G5   D/F#   Cadd9   G5
As it was in the be - ginning, is now until the end.

Em   G5   D/F#
Woman draws her life ___ from man and gives it back again,

       Cadd9   G5   Gsus4 G A Asus2
And there is love, there is ___ love.

| C Cmaj7 C6 | C | G5 Gsus4 G |

Bridge

             C*   C/B   Am7
Well, then what's to be ___ the rea - son

Am7/G D/F#   G
For be - coming man and wife?

Gsus4 C*   C/B   Am7
Is it love that brings you here,

Am7/G D/F#   G
Or love that brings you life?

Verse 3

Gsus4 G5   D/F#   Cadd9   G5
For if loving is the an - swer, then who's the giving for?

   Em   G5   D/F#
Do you believe in some - thing that you've never seen before?

       Cadd9   G5 Gsus4 G A Asus2
Oh, there's love, oh, there's love.

| C Cmaj7 C6 | C | G5 Gsus4 G | Gsus4 |

Interlude

| G5 Gsus4 | G | D/F# | |
| Em | G5 | D/F# | |

Verse 4

      G5   D/F#   Cadd9   G5
Oh, the marraige of your spirits here has caused Him to remain,

         Em   G5   D/F#
For when - ever two or more of you are gathered in His name

       Cadd9   G5   Gsus4 G A Asus2
There is love, ah, there's ___ love.

| C Cmaj7 C6 | C | G5 Gsus4 G | G* ‖

When You Say Nothing at All

Words and Music by
Don Schlitz and Paul Overstreet

Melody:

It's a-maz - ing how _ you   can speak right _

(Capo 1st fret)

D   A   G   G/B   A/C#

1 3 2   1 2 3   3 2 4   2   4   3 1 1 1

Intro

| D   A | G   A | D   A | G   A | |

Verse 1

D   A   G   A   D A G A
  It's amaz - ing how you   can speak right ___ to my heart.

D   A   G   A   D A G A
  Without say - ing a word ___ you can light up the dark.

G   A
Try as I may I could nev - er explain

D   A   G   A
  What I hear ___ when you don't ___ say a thing.

Chorus 1

     D   A
The smile on your face

        G   A
Lets me know ___ that you need ___ me.

      D   A
There's a truth in your eyes

      G   A
Saying you'll ___ never leave ___ me.

    D   A
A touch of your hand

      G   A G/B A/C#
Says you'll catch ___ me if ev - er I fall.

  G   A
Now you say it best   when you say nothing at all.

Interlude 1	*Repeat Intro*

Verse 2

D   A   G   A   D A G A
All day long ____ I can hear   people talk - ing out loud,

D   A   G   A   D A G A
But when you __ hold me near __ you drown out the crowd.

G   A
Old Mister Webster could nev - er define

D   A   G   A
What's being said ___ between your ___ heart and mine.

Chorus 2	*Repeat Chorus 1*

Interlude 2

|D   A |G   A |D   A |G |
|D   A |G |A |G |

Chorus 3	*Repeat Chorus 1*

Outro

‖: D   A |G   :‖ *Repeat and fade*

You and I

Words and Music by
Frank Myers

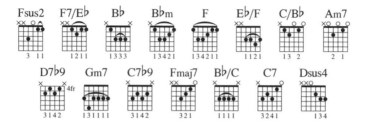

Intro

‖: **Fsus2** | :‖

Verse 1

Fsus2   **F7/E♭**   **B♭**
  Just you and I,   sharing our love ____ together,

Fsus2   **F7/E♭**   **B♭**
  And I know in time   we'll build the dreams ____ we treasure.

B♭m   **F**   **B♭m**   **Fsus2**
  And we'll be all right ____   just you and I.

Verse 2   *Repeat Verse 1*

Bridge

E♭/F F   B♭ C/B♭   Am7
    And I re - member our first embrace,

  D7♭9   Gm7
That smile that was on your face,

  C7♭9   Fmaj7
The promises that we made.

E♭/F F   B♭ C/B♭   Am7
    And now, your love is my reward,

  D7♭9   Gm7   B♭/C   Fsus2
And I love you even more ___ than I ever did ___ before.

Verse 3

Fsus2   F7/E♭   B♭
  Just you and I,   we care and trust ___ each other.

Fsus2   F7/E♭   B♭
  With you in my life,   there'll never be ___ another.

B♭m   F B♭m   Fsus2
  We'll be all right ___   just you and I.

Outro

E♭/F F   B♭ C/B♭   Am7
    And I re - member our first embrace,

  D7♭9   Gm7
That smile that was on your face,

  C7♭9   Fmaj7
The promises that we made.

E♭/F F   B♭ C/B♭   Am7
    And now, your love is my reward,

  D7♭9   Gm7   C7♭9   C7   Am7 Dsus4 D7♭9
And I love you even more ___ than I ever did ___ before.

Gm7   B♭/C Fsus2
We made it, you and I.

You Are the Sunshine of My Life

Words and Music by
Stevie Wonder

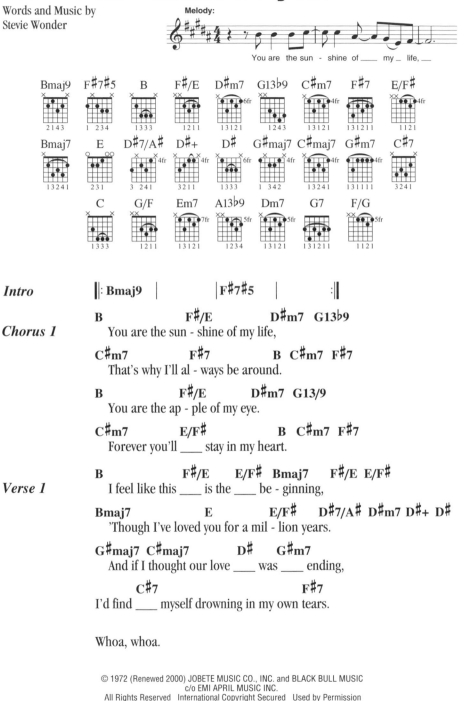

Intro

‖: Bmaj9 | | F#7#5 | :‖

Chorus 1

B   F#/E   D#m7 G13♭9
You are the sun - shine of my life,

C#m7   F#7   B C#m7 F#7
That's why I'll al - ways be around.

B   F#/E   D#m7 G13/9
You are the ap - ple of my eye.

C#m7   E/F#   B C#m7 F#7
Forever you'll ____ stay in my heart.

Verse 1

B   F#/E   E/F# Bmaj7   F#/E E/F#
I feel like this ____ is the ____ be - ginning,

Bmaj7   E   E/F#   D#7/A# D#m7 D#+ D#
'Though I've loved you for a mil - lion years.

G#maj7 C#maj7   D#   G#m7
And if I thought our love ____ was ____ ending,

        C#7   F#7
I'd find ____ myself drowning in my own tears.

Whoa, whoa.

Chorus 2

B   F#/E   D#m7 G13♭9
You are the sun - shine of my life,

C#m7   F#7   B C#m7 F#7
That's why I'll al - ways stay around.

B   F#/E   D#m7 G13♭9
You are the ap - ple of my eye.

C#m7   E/F#   B C#m7 F#7
Forever you ____ stay in my heart.

Verse 2

B   F#/E   E/F# Bmaj7   F#/E E/F#
You must have known ____ that I ____ was ____ lonely,

Bmaj7   E   E/F#   D#7/A# D#m7 D#+ D#
Because you came ____ to my ____ rescue.

G#maj7   C#maj7   D#   G#m7
And I know that his must ____ be ____ heaven.

          C#7   F#7
How could so ____ much love be inside of you?

G7
Whoa,

Chorus 3

   C   G/F   Em7 A13♭9
‖: You are the sun - shine of my life,

Dm7   G7   C Dm7 G7
That's why I'll al - ways stay around.

C   G/F   Em7 A13♭9
You are the ap - ple of my eye.

Dm7   F/G   C Dm7 G7
Forever you ____ stay in my heart.   :‖ *Repeat and fade*

You Decorated My Life

Words and Music by
Debbie Hupp and Bob Morrison

All my life was a pa - per

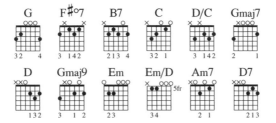

| G | F#°7 | B7 | C | D/C | Gmaj7 |
| D | Gmaj9 | Em | Em/D | Am7 | D7 |

Intro |G |F#°7 B7 |C D/C C | D/C C |

Verse 1
         G   **C**
All my life was a paper once plain, pure and white,

          Gmaj7
Till you moved with your pen changin' moods now and then

          C
Till the balance was right.

          G   **C**
Then you added music, ev'ry note was in place

          Gmaj7
And any - body could see all the changes in me

          C
By the look on my face.

Chorus 1

D C D   G Gmaj9 C   G Gmaj9
    And you _____ decorated my life,

C   B7   Em Em/D   Am7 D7
  Cre - ated a world   where dreams are a part.

  G Gmaj9 C   G Gmaj9
And you _____ decorated my life

C   B7   Em Em/D   Am7
  By paintin' your love   all over my heart,

D7   G F#°7 B7 C D/C C D/C C
  You decorated my life.

Verse 2

      G   C
Like a rhyme with no reason in an unfinished song,

    Gmaj7
There was no harmony, life meant nothing to me,

    C
Until you came along.

     G   C
And you brought out the colors, what a gentle surprise.

    Gmaj7
Now I'm able to see all the things life can be,

    C
Shining soft in your eyes.

Chorus 2

D C D   G Gmaj9 C   G Gmaj9
    And you _____ decorated my life,

C   B7   Em Em/D   Am7 D7
  Cre - ated a world ____ where dreams are a part.

  G Gmaj9 C   G Gmaj9
And you _____ decorated my life

C   B7   Em Em/D   Am7
  By painting your love ____ all over my heart,

D7   G F#°7 B7 C D/C C D/C C Gmaj7
  You decorated my life.

You Light Up My Life

Words and Music by
Joseph Brooks

Melody:

So man - y nights I'd sit by __

Am   D   G   Em   F#m7   B7   E7   D/F#   F#   A7

Dmaj7   D7   Em7   A/C#   Bm   E   D/A   Dsus4/A   A

Intro |Am | |

Verse 1

Am   D   G   Em
So many nights I'd sit by my window

F#m7   B7   Em   E7
Waiting for someone to sing me his song.

Am   D   G   D/F#   Em
So many dreams I kept deep ___ in - side me,

F#   A7
A - lone in the dark, but now you've come along.

Chorus 1

D Dmaj7   D7
And you light up my life.

B7   Em
You give me hope to carry on.

Em7   A7
You light up my days

D A/C# Bm   Em   A7
And fill my nights _____ with ___ song.

Verse 2

Am   D   G   Em
Rollin' at sea, a - drift on the water,

F#m7   B7   Em   E7
Could it be fin'lly I'm turning for home?

Am   D   G   D/F# Em
Fin'lly a chance to say, "Hey! ___ I love you."

F#   A7
Never again to be all alone.

Chorus 2   *Repeat Chorus 1*

Outro-Chorus

      D   Dmaj7   D7
'Cause you, you light up my life.

        B7   Em
You give me hope to carry on.

    Em7   A7
You light up my days

        F#   Bm
And fill my nights with song.

E   D   F#   Bm
It can't be wrong when it feels so right,

E   D/A Dsus4/A A
 'Cause you

   G D A G D
You light up my life.

You Raise Me Up

Words and Music by
Brendan Graham and
Rolf Lovland

Melody:

When I am down and, oh, _ my soul's so wear-y, _____

(Capo 1st fret)

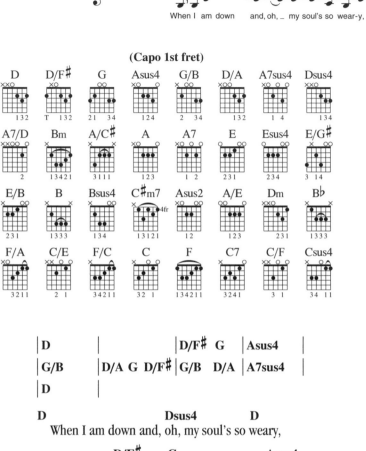

Intro

D			D/F♯ G	Asus4	
G/B	D/A G D/F♯	G/B D/A	A7sus4	
D					

Verse

D   Dsus4   D
When I am down and, oh, my soul's so weary,

      D/F♯ G   Asus4
When troubles come and my heart burdened be,

     G   D/F♯
Then I am still and wait here in the silence

G   D   A7/D   D
Until you come and sit a while with me.

Chorus 1

        Bm   G   D/F#
You raise me up so I can stand on mountains.

A/C#   Bm G   D/F#
  You raise me up to walk on stormy seas.

A   D   G/B   D/A   D/F#
  I am strong when I am on your shoul - ders.

G   D/A A7   D
  You raise me up to more than I can be.

Interlude

| E Esus4 | E | E/G# A | E/B B |
| A/C# A | E/G# A | E/B Bsus4 | E |

Chorus 2

               C#m7 A   E/G#
You raise me up so   I can stand on mountains.

B   C#m7 A   E/B
  You raise me up to   walk on stormy seas.

B   E
  I am strong when I am on your shoulders.

Asus2   E/B Bsus4   E A/E E
  You raise me up to more than I can ___ be.

Chorus 3

N.C.   Dm Bb   F/A
You raise me up so I can stand on mountains.

C/E   Dm Bb   F/C
  You raise me up to walk on stormy seas.

C   F   Bb   F
  I am strong when I am on your shoulders.

Bb   F/C C7   F
  You raise me up to more than I can be.

Outro-Chorus

A7   Dm Bb   F/A
  You raise me up so I can stand on mountains.

C/E   Dm Bb   F/C
  You raise me up to walk on stormy seas.

C   F   C/F   F
  I am strong when I am on your shoulders.

Bb   F/C Csus4   Dm Bb
  You raise me up to more than I can be.

N.C.   F/C C7   Bb C/F F
You raise me up to more than I can ___ be.

Guitar Chord Songbooks

Each book includes complete lyrics, chord symbols, and guitar chord diagrams.

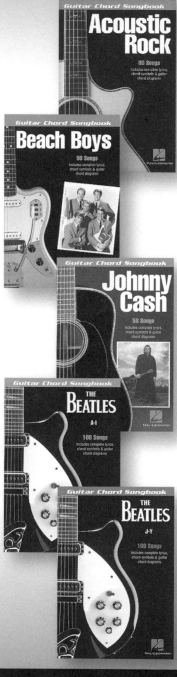

Acoustic Rock
80 acoustic favorites: Blackbird • Blowin' in the Wind • Layla • Maggie May • Me and Julio down by the Schoolyard • Pink Houses • and more.
00699540.. $17.95

Alabama
50 of Alabama's best: Born Country • Dixieland Delight • Feels So Right • Mountain Music • Song of the South • Why Lady Why • and more.
00699914 .... $14.95

The Beach Boys
59 favorites: California Girls • Don't Worry Baby • Fun, Fun, Fun • Good Vibrations • Help Me Rhonda • Wouldn't It Be Nice • dozens more!
00699566.. $14.95

Blues
80 blues tunes: Big Boss Man • Cross Road Blues (Crossroads) • Damn Right, I've Got the Blues • Pride and Joy • Route 66 • Sweet Home Chicago • and more.
00699733 .... $12.95

Broadway
80 stage hits: All I Ask of You • Bali Ha'i • Edelweiss • Hello, Dolly! • Memory • Ol' Man River • People • Seasons of Love • Sunrise, Sunset • and more.
00699920 .... $14.99

Johnny Cash
58 Cash classics: A Boy Named Sue • Cry, Cry, Cry • Daddy Sang Bass • Folsom Prison Blues • I Walk the Line • Ring of Fire • Solitary Man • and more.
00699648.. $16.95

The Beatles (A-I)
An awesome reference of Beatles hits: All You Need Is Love • The Ballad of John and Yoko • Get Back • Good Day Sunshine • A Hard Day's Night • Hey Jude • I Saw Her Standing There • and more!
00699558.. $17.99

The Beatles (J-Y)
100 more Beatles hits: Lady Madonna • Let It Be • Ob-La-Di, Ob-La-Da • Paperback Writer • Revolution • Twist and Shout • When I'm Sixty-Four • and more.
00699562.. $17.99

Steven Curtis Chapman
65 from this CCM superstar: Be Still and Know • Cinderella • For the Sake of the Call • Live Out Loud • Speechless • With Hope • and more.
00700702 .... $14.99

Children's Songs
70 songs for kids: Alphabet Song • Bingo • The Candy Man • Eensy Weensy Spider • Puff the Magic Dragon • Twinkle, Twinkle Little Star • and more!
00699539.. $14.95

Complete contents listings available online at www.halleonard.com

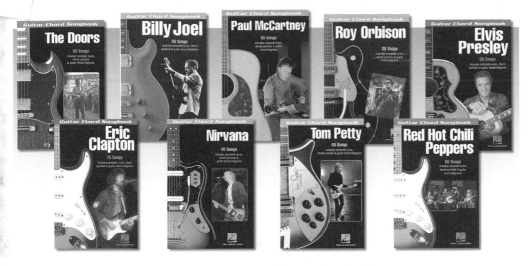

Christmas Carols
80 Christmas carols: Angels We Have Heard on High • The Holly and the Ivy • I Saw Three Ships • Joy to the World • O Holy Night • Silent Night • What Child Is This? • and more.
00699536...$12.95

Christmas Songs
80 Christmas favorites: The Christmas Song • Feliz Navidad • Jingle-Bell Rock • Merry Christmas, Darling • Rudolph the Red-Nosed Reindeer • more.
00699537...$12.95

Eric Clapton
75 of Slowhand's finest: I Shot the Sheriff • Knockin' on Heaven's Door • Layla • Strange Brew • Tears in Heaven • Wonderful Tonight • and more!
00699567...$15.99

Classic Rock
80 rock essentials: Beast of Burden • Cat Scratch Fever • Hot Blooded • Money • Rhiannon • Sweet Emotion • Walk on the Wild Side • more
00699598...$15.99

Contemporary Christian
80 hits from today's top CCM artists: Awesome God • El Shaddai • Friends • His Strength Is Perfect • I Will Be Here • A Maze of Grace • Run to You • more.
00699564...$14.95

Country
80 country standards: Boot Scootin' Boogie • Crazy • Hey, Good Lookin'• Sixteen Tons • Through the Years • Your Cheatin' Heart • more.
00699534...$14.95

Country Favorites
Over 60 songs: Achy Breaky Heart (Don't Tell My Heart) • Brand New Man • Gone Country • The Long Black Veil • Make the World Go Away • and more.
00700609 ....$14.99

Country Standards
60 songs: By the Time I Get to Phoenix • El Paso • The Gambler • I Fall to Pieces • Jolene • King of the Road • Put Your Hand in the Hand • A Rainy Night in Georgia • more.
00700608 ....$12.95

Cowboy Songs
Over 60 tunes: Back in the Saddle Again • Happy Trails • Home on the Range • Streets of Laredo • The Yellow Rose of Texas • and more.
00699636...$12.95

The Doors
60 classics. Break on Through to the Other Side • The End • L.A. Woman • Light My Fire • Love Her Madly • Love Me Two Times • People Are Strange • Riders on the Storm • Twentieth Century Fox • and more.
00699888 ....$15.99

Early Rock
80 early rock classics: All I Have to Do Is Dream • Fever • He's So Fine • I'm Sorry • Lollipop • Puppy Love • Sh-Boom (Life Could Be a Dream) • and more.
00699916 ....$14.99

Folk Pop Rock
80 songs: American Pie • Dust in the Wind • Me and Bobby McGee • Somebody to Love • Time in a Bottle • and more.
00699651...$14.95

Folksongs
80 folk favorites: Aura Lee • Camptown Races • Danny Boy • Man of Constant Sorrow • Nobody Knows the Trouble I've Seen • When the Saints Go Marching In • and more.
00699541...$12.95

Gospel Hymns
80 hymns: Amazing Grace • Give Me That Old Time Religion • I Love to Tell the Story • The Old Rugged Cross • Shall We Gather at the River? • Wondrous Love • and more.
00700463 ....$14.99

For more information, see your local music dealer or visit www.halleonard.com

Grand Ole Opry®
80 great songs: Abilene • Act Naturally • Country Boy • Crazy • Friends in Low Places • He Stopped Loving Her Today • Wings of a Dove • dozens more!
00699885 ....$16.95

Hillsong United
65 top worship songs: Break Free • Everyday • From the Inside Out • God Is Great • Look to You • Now That You're Near • Salvation Is Here • To the Ends of the Earth • and more.
00700222 ....$12.95

Jazz Standards
50 songs: Ain't Misbehavin' • Cheek to Cheek • In the Wee Small Hours of the Morning • The Nearness of You • Stardust • The Way You Look Tonight • and more.
00700972 ....$14.95

Billy Joel
60 Billy Joel favorites: • It's Still Rock and Roll to Me • The Longest Time • Piano Man • She's Always a Woman • Uptown Girl • We Didn't Start the Fire • You May Be Right • and more.
00699632..$15.99

Elton John
60 songs: Bennie and the Jets • Candle in the Wind • Crocodile Rock • Goodbye Yellow Brick Road • Pinball Wizard • Sad Songs (Say So Much) • Tiny Dancer • Your Song • and more.
00699732 ....$15.99

Latin
60 favorites: Bésame Mucho (Kiss Me Much) • The Girl from Ipanema (Garôta De Ipanema) • The Look of Love • So Nice (Summer Samba) • and more.
00700973 ....$14.95

Paul McCartney
60 from Sir Paul: Band on the Run • Jet • Let 'Em In • Maybe I'm Amazed • No More Lonely Nights • Say Say Say • Take It Away • With a Little Luck • more!
00385035 ....$16.95

Motown
60 Motown masterpieces: ABC • Baby I Need Your Lovin' • I'll Be There • Just My Imagination • Lady Marmalade • Stop! In the Name of Love • You Can't Hurry Love • more.
00699734 ....$16.95

The 1950s
80 early rock favorites: High Hopes • Mister Sandman • Only You (And You Alone) • Put Your Head on My Shoulder • Que Sera, Sera (Whatever Will Be, Will Be) • Tammy • That's Amoré • and more.
00699922 ....$14.99

The 1980s
80 hits: Centerfold • Come on Eileen • Don't Worry, Be Happy • Got My Mind Set on You • Sailing • Should I Stay or Should I Go • Sweet Dreams (Are Made of This) • more.
00700551 ....$16.99

Nirvana
40 songs: About a Girl • Come as You Are • Heart Shaped Box • The Man Who Sold the World • Smells like Teen Spirit • You Know You're Right • and more.
00699762 ....$16.99

Roy Orbison
38 songs: Blue Bayou • Crying • Oh, Pretty Woman • Only the Lonely (Know the Way I Feel) • Pretty Paper • Running Scared • Working for the Man • You Got It • and more.
00699752 ....$12.95

Tom Petty
American Girl • Breakdown • Don't Do Me like That • Free Fallin' • Here Comes My Girl • Into the Great Wide Open • Mary Jane's Last Dance • Refugee • Runnin' Down a Dream • The Waiting • more.
00699883 ....$15.99

Pop/Rock
80 chart hits: Against All Odds • Come Sail Away • Every Breath You Take • Hurts So Good • Kokomo • More Than Words • Smooth • Summer of '69 • and more.
00699538..$14.95

Praise and Worship
80 favorites: Agnus Dei • He Is Exalted • I Could Sing of Your Love Forever • Lord, I Lift Your Name on High • More Precious Than Silver • Open the Eyes of My Heart • Shine, Jesus, Shine • and more.
00699634 ....$12.95

Elvis Presley
60 hits: All Shook Up • Blue Suede Shoes • Can't Help Falling in Love • Heartbreak Hotel • Hound Dog • Jailhouse Rock • Suspicious Minds • Viva Las Vegas • more.
00699633..$14.95

Red Hot Chili Peppers
50 hits: Breaking the Girl • By the Way • Californication • Give It Away • Higher Ground • Love Rollercoaster • Scar Tissue • Suck My Kiss • Under the Bridge • What It Is • and more.
00699710..$16.95

Rock 'n' Roll
80 rock 'n' roll classics: At the Hop • Great Balls of Fire • It's My Party • La Bamba • My Boyfriend's Back • Peggy Sue • Stand by Me • more.
00699535..$14.95

Sting
50 favorites from Sting and the Police: Brand New Day • Can't Stand Losing You • Don't Stand So Close to Me • Every Breath You Take • Fields of Gold • King of Pain • Message in a Bottle • Roxanne • more.
00699921 ....$14.99

Three Chord Songs
65 includes: All Right Now • La Bamba • Lay Down Sally • Mony, Mony • Rock Around the Clock • Rock This Town • Werewolves of London • You Are My Sunshine • and more.
00699720 ....$12.95

HAL•LEONARD®